Exploring the Solar System

Bruce LaFontaine

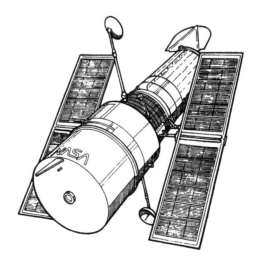

DOVER PUBLICATIONS, INC.
Mineola, New York

DEDICATION
To Carl Sagan
Scientist, Educator, Cosmic Visionary
1934–1996

"We are made of Star Stuff"

Copyright

Copyright © 1998 by Bruce LaFontaine
All rights reserved under Pan American and International Copyright Conventions.

Bibliographical Note

Exploring the Solar System is a new work, first published by Dover Publications, Inc., in 1998.

DOVER *Pictorial Archive* SERIES

This book belongs to the Dover Pictorial Archive Series. You may use the designs and illustrations for graphics and crafts applications, free and without special permission, provided that you include no more than ten in the same publication or project. (For permission for additional use, please write to Permissions Department, Dover Publications, Inc., 31 East 2nd Street, Mineola, N.Y. 11501.)
However, republication or reproduction of any illustration by any other graphic service, whether it be in a book or in any other design resource, is strictly prohibited.

International Standard Book Number: 0-486-40361-0

Manufactured in the United States of America
Dover Publications, Inc., 31 East 2nd Street, Mineola, N.Y. 11501

Introduction

Human civilization has been fascinated with the starry heavens since ancient times. Structures and monuments built for the sole purpose of observing them have been found in Europe, Africa, Asia, and the Americas; they date from the dawn of mankind. This study of the planets, moons, and stars is called astronomy. It is one of the oldest scientific endeavors, with astronomical records dating back to 3000 B.C. Early astronomers made remarkably accurate observations and calculations without the aid of the telescope or other sophisticated instruments. The invention of the telescope in 1609 was a milestone in the history of astronomy, leading to a wealth of new information about the planets and stars.

Modern astronomers primarily use two types of instruments to study celestial objects: optical telescopes and radio telescopes. Optical telescopes gather and focus light from objects in the night sky using mirrors and lenses to magnify these images. There are two kinds of optical telescopes, reflectors and refractors. Radio telescopes, invented in the mid-twentieth century, use large radio antenna dishes to receive types of radiation other than light emitted by celestial bodies, such as radio waves, x-rays, and gamma rays.

Since the 1960s, scientists have also used robotic space probes launched from the earth to gather information about the various planets and moons of the solar system. These robot spacecraft have flown close to, orbited, and photographed all of the planets except for distant Pluto. Several have actually landed on Venus and Mars, relaying close-up photos of the surfaces of these worlds.

From their research, astronomers know that the earth is part of a solar system, one of nine planets orbiting a medium-sized yellow-white star we call the sun. Earth is the third planet from this star. The four planets closest to the sun are called the "terrestrial planets," after our own planet earth. They are Mercury, Venus, Earth, and Mars, and they have solid rocky surfaces. Farther from the sun are the outer "gas giant" planets of Jupiter, Saturn, Uranus, and Neptune. These planets are massive spheres of gas—mainly hydrogen and helium—with small inner cores of liquid metallic elements, but no solid surface. The gas giants have numerous moons orbiting them, some as large as planets. These moons consist mostly of rock and ice. The most distant planet is Pluto; it is also the smallest. Little is known about it because of its immense distance from earth. It may be an unusual type of planet known as an "icy dwarf."

Other members of our solar system are the asteroids and the periodic comets. Asteroids are rocky fragments—some as large as small moons—left over from the formation of the solar system. They orbit the sun in a wide belt between the planets Mars and Jupiter. Comets are frozen balls of ice and rock that circle the sun in great elliptical orbits that bring them close to the earth over regular but lengthy periods of time. They originate in a vast accumulation called the "Oort cloud," which lies far beyond the orbit of the planet Pluto.

Beyond our solar system lies a larger collection of stars called the Milky Way galaxy, and we are located on one of the outer spiral arms of this vast assemblage of stars. Our galaxy is but one of billions in the known universe. The study of planets, moons, and stars is not only a fascinating subject, but it is also a reflection of mankind's strong desire to explore new territory and gain a greater understanding of our place in the universe.

STONEHENGE (circa 2000 B.C.)

Many ancient civilizations observed and studied the night skies, constructing monuments to help them view and record celestial events such as comets, eclipses, and novae (exploding stars). The remains of these primitive observatories can be found in Greece, China, Arabia, North and South America, and Europe.

The most famous, elaborate, and well-preserved of these early astronomical sites is a circle of standing stones on the Salisbury Plain of England known as Stonehenge. It was built by the native inhabitants of Britain during three periods of construction and reconstruction (c. 1800 B.C.–1400 B.C.), predating the arrival of the Romans and Danes in the British Isles. Stonehenge was believed to be a primitive calendar device for observing, recording, and celebrating celestial and seasonal events

like the annual onset of summer and winter—known as the "solstice"—which had great significance to these agrarian societies.

Stonehenge consists of an outer circle of thirty vertical stones, called the "Sarsen Circle." Each stone is about thirteen and one-half feet tall and weighs approximately twenty-five tons. These are topped by horizontal stones called "lintels." The diameter of this outer ring is ninety-seven feet. There is also an inner ring of smaller stones called "bluestones." Outside the main circle is a single "heelstone," which probably served as a focal point for sighting the rising sun. Since the stone quarries for the Stonehenge monuments are many miles distant, the technology and means by which a primitive Bronze Age people moved and erected these massive structures is still a mystery.

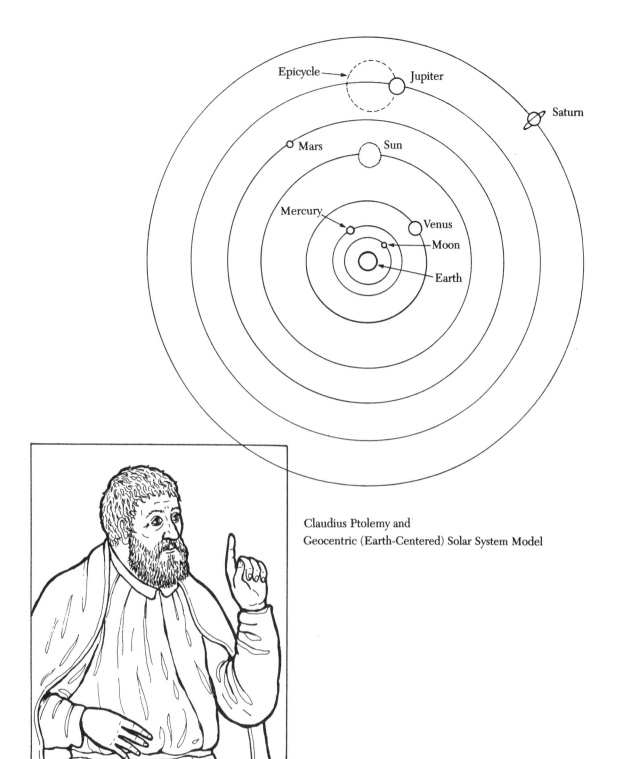

Claudius Ptolemy and
Geocentric (Earth-Centered) Solar System Model

PTOLEMAIC SYSTEM (circa A.D. 150)

The Greek astronomer, Claudius Ptolemy*, was the first to devise a widely accepted system or model to explain the motion of the earth and other heavenly bodies. His book, *The Almagest*, described the solar system as "geocentric," meaning earth-centered. He believed that the sun, moon, and planets all revolved around the earth in perfect circles, which readily explained the apparent motion of the sun and moon, but not the planets.

In general, early astronomers observed the planets as becoming brighter and dimmer in regular cycles, as well as wandering or wobbling against the background of the stars, which were set in their fixed positions. In fact, the Greek word *planetes* means "wanderer." The planets also appeared to stop and travel backward from time to time, a phenomenon called "retrograde" motion. Of course, the planets do not actually move backward. We know now that Ptolemy perceived the planets orbiting the sun in elliptical, not circular, paths. When the earth

orbited the sun, and passed one of the planets in its orbit, that planet would appear to be traveling backward.

Ptolemy invented a complicated explanation to solve the riddle of this apparent backward planetary motion to further support his geocentric theory. He postulated that the planets revolved around the earth in large circular orbits; and additionally, along those circles, rotated in smaller circles which he called "epicycles." To the ancient Greeks, this was a satisfactory explanation for the observed brightening-dimming effect of the planets and their peculiar motion. This incorrect geocentric model of the solar system would prevail as scientific fact for the next 1,300 years. This concept was finally shattered by the work of the great Polish astronomer, Copernicus, in the year 1543.

*HISTORICAL NOTE: The Greek astronomer, Claudius Ptolemy, should not be confused with the numerous pharaohs of the Ptolemy dynasty who ruled Egypt many centuries earlier.

Nicolaus Copernicus

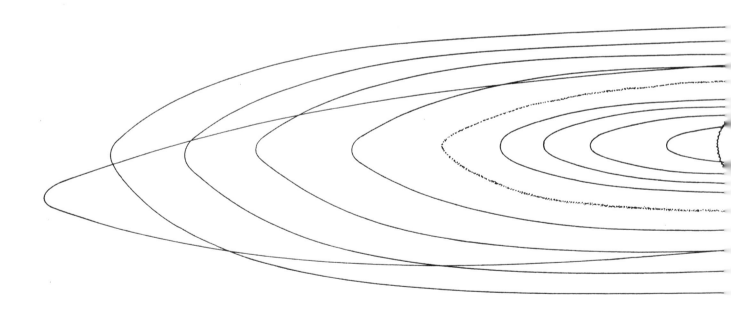

COPERNICAN REVOLUTION (A.D. 1543)

Nicolaus Copernicus (1473–1543) is considered the founder of modern astronomy by many historians and scientists. He conceived the theory that the planets revolved around the sun, not the earth—the "heliocentric" model of the solar system—in his landmark book, *On the Revolution of Celestial Spheres*, published in 1543.

Copernicus was born in 1473 in the town of Torun, Poland. He was raised by his uncle, Lukasz, a prominent bishop in the Catholic Church. He was educated in law and medicine at a number of European universities. With the help of his uncle, he was appointed to the position of "canon" (or business manager) of the Church at the age of 24. He began his observation and study of the night sky in 1512.

Copernicus' model of the solar system was not without error. Although he correctly stated that the sun is the center of our solar system, he still had the planets revolving around the sun in perfectly circular orbits, with smaller epicycles, as in Ptolemy's work. Despite this flaw, his studies became the foundation for the research of many other scientists, including the four great astronomers of the Renaissance: Tycho Brahe, Johannes Kepler, Galileo Galilei, and Isaac Newton.

Mercury　　Venus　　Earth　　Mars　　Asteroids　　Jupiter　　Saturn　　Uranus　Neptune　　Pluto

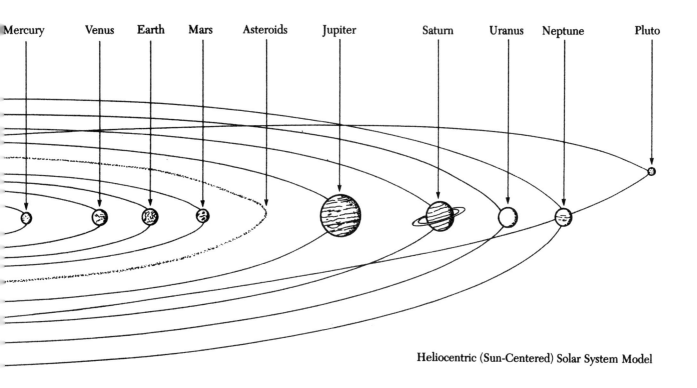

Heliocentric (Sun-Centered) Solar System Model

Tycho

Kepler

Astronomical Sextant

Kepler's Laws of Planetary Motion

Sun

Perihelion

Aphelion

TYCHO BRAHE (1546–1601) and JOHANNES KEPLER (1571–1630)

The two great astronomers of the early Renaissance period were Tycho Brahe, and his student, Johannes Kepler, whose studies were crucial to a greater understanding of the nature of our solar system.

Tycho (commonly referred to by his first name only) established the first large and dedicated astronomical observatory in Europe. In 1576, on the Danish island of Hveen, he began to observe and chart the position and movements of the sun, moon, planets, and stars. Without the aid of a telescope—which had not yet been invented—he relied upon his own hand-crafted instruments, such as the quadrant and astronomi-

cal sextant, shown above. He is regarded as the foremost observational astronomer of his era.

Tycho's pupil, Johannes Kepler, was the finest mathematical astronomer of the period. In 1619, his studies were published in the book, *Harmony of the World*, wherein he correctly calculated the paths of the planets in their orbit around the sun. These calculations are now known as "Kepler's Laws of Planetary Motion." He is also credited with writing the first science fiction book, *Somnium* ("Dreams"), in 1608.

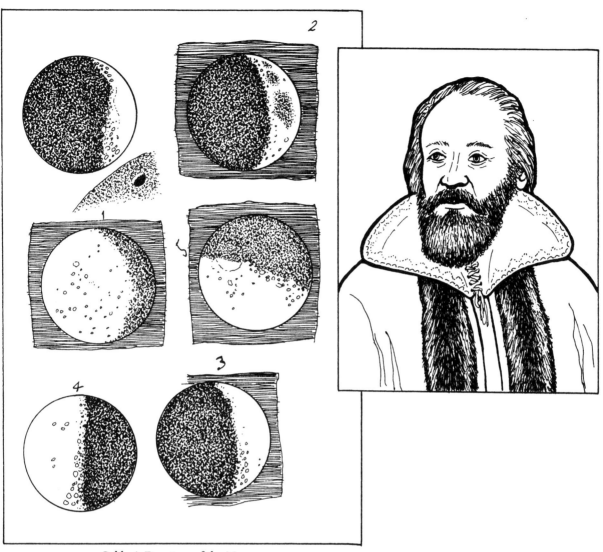

Galileo's Drawings of the Moon

Refractor Telescope

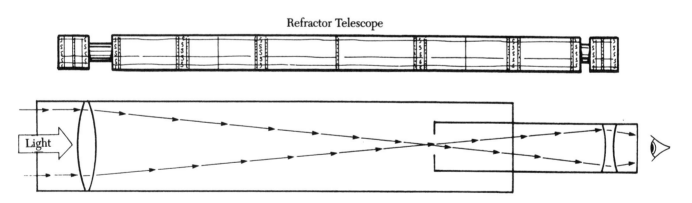

Light

GALILEO GALILEI (1564–1642)

The Italian-born Galileo Galilei was one of the greatest scientists of the Renaissance era. Improving upon a telescope design by Dutch optician Hans Lippershey, Galileo used his hand-crafted refracting telescope to see craters, mountains, and great plains on the surface of the moon—known as "seas." Galileo also discovered four large moons orbiting the planet Jupiter; commonly referred to as the Galilean satellites, they are now named Ganymede, Callisto, Io, and Europa.

The type of telescope constructed and used by Galileo is a "refracting" telescope, because the glass lenses in the telescope tube "refract," or bend, light as it passes through them. It is this bending which causes the magnification of an image as seen by the viewer. The refracting tele-

scope was widely used until the late nineteenth century, when the "reflecting" telescope (see page 10) became more popular.

Galileo, a prominent figure of his time and place, was an outspoken advocate of the still controversial notion that the sun is at the center of the solar system, believing that his own telescopic observations confirmed this theory of the great astronomer, Copernicus. Since his endorsement of this system stood in direct opposition to the Catholic Church's doctrine of a geocentric universe, Galileo was censured by the Church; facing trial and possible execution by the Inquisition, he wisely recanted.

Isaac Newton invents Reflector Telescope, 1668

Light

ISAAC NEWTON (1642–1727)

Isaac Newton is revered by the scientific community as one of the great geniuses in human history, who—along with such others as Albert Einstein—helped transform our knowledge of the physical universe.

Newton studied and taught at the Trinity College of Cambridge University in England. He was a mathematician who was drawn to astronomy by his interest in the properties of light. He used a glass prism to separate white light into its constituent colors of red, orange, yellow, blue, green, and violet. In 1668, Newton invented the reflecting telescope, which uses highly polished mirrors to collect and reflect light through a magnifying eyepiece. The huge optical telescopes used by modern observatories are based on this same technology.

Isaac Newton's greatest discoveries were published in his book, *Principia Mathematica* (*Principles of Mathematics*), in the year 1686. In this volume, through brilliantly conceived mathematical equations, Newton describes the laws of force and motion, and the movement of planetary bodies—including the speed needed to break free of the earth's gravity. He also presents his stunning revelations about the nature of gravity as one of the four elemental forces of the universe (along with electromagnetism, the strong nuclear force, and the weak nuclear force, the latter two relating to the nature of infinitesimally small atomic particles). In general, Newton's impact on modern science and mathematics—especially calculus—can never be overestimated.

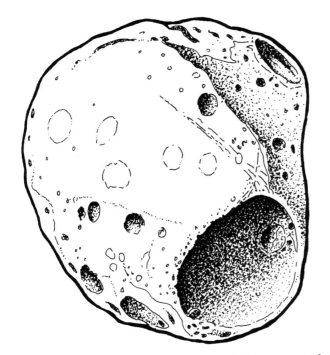
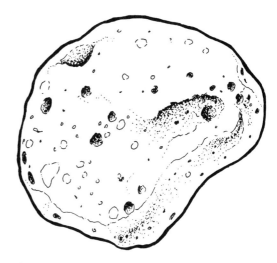

Martian moons, Phobos (left) and Deimos (right)

ASAPH HALL (1829–1907)

The year 1877 was a memorable one in the history of astronomy as new discoveries about the planet Mars made headlines in the world's newspapers. Public perception of the "red planet" would never be the same.

An American astronomer, Asaph Hall, discovered the existence of two tiny, irregularly shaped moons circling Mars while viewing the planet at the U.S. Naval Observatory. The moons were named Phobos (fear) and Deimos (terror), after the horses and charioteers that accompanied the Roman God of War, Mars. Phobos, the larger moon, orbits Mars at a distance of 5,760 miles. It is roughly twelve miles by fourteen miles by seventeen miles in size. Deimos orbits Mars at a distance of 14,540 miles, and its size is approximately six miles by seven miles by nine miles.

Also in 1877, Italian astronomer Giovanni Schiaparelli (1835–1910)

believed that he saw markings on the surface of Mars which appeared to be *canali* (or channels). His findings were incorrectly translated into English so that channels became "canals," a word that strongly connotes artificial construction and the suggestion of intelligent Martian life. This erroneous impression of Mars remained fixed in the public consciousness until the explorations of U.S. spacecraft Mariner 4 in 1965 found that the markings first observed in 1877 were actually craters. Despite the fact that there is no evidence to indicate that intelligent life on Mars has ever existed, it continues to inspire the popular imagination in that regard more than any other planet. Mars is also currently the object of many scientific programs, including robot orbiters and landers, as well as an eventual manned mission to the planet.

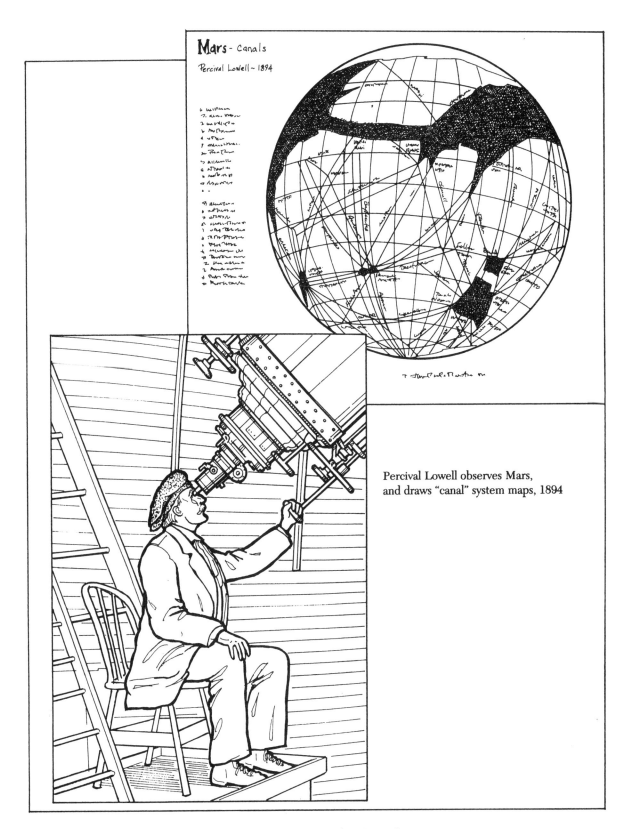

Percival Lowell observes Mars,
and draws "canal" system maps, 1894

PERCIVAL LOWELL (1855–1916)

Because of Schiaparelli's claims in 1877, Mars became the object of intense scrutiny by astronomers. In 1894, American astronomer Percival Lowell further supported those claims by maintaining that he too had observed the Martian canals. He theorized that the planet was inhabited by a dying civilization struggling to survive on its harsh desert planet by transporting water from the north and solar polar ice caps through a vast network of canals and pumping stations. Lowell's drawings of this alleged Martian canal system were even more detailed than Schiaparelli's, showing 184 major canals—twice as many as the Italian astronomer observed.

Percival Lowell established an observatory in the mountains near Flagstaff, Arizona. He devoted his life to observing the red planet with a twenty-four inch refracting telescope, peering through the clear skies of the high desert. Concluding that he saw what he wanted to see and not what really existed, other astronomers did not support Lowell's theories about the Martian surface. Nevertheless, he helped fuel the intense interest in Mars which continues to this day.

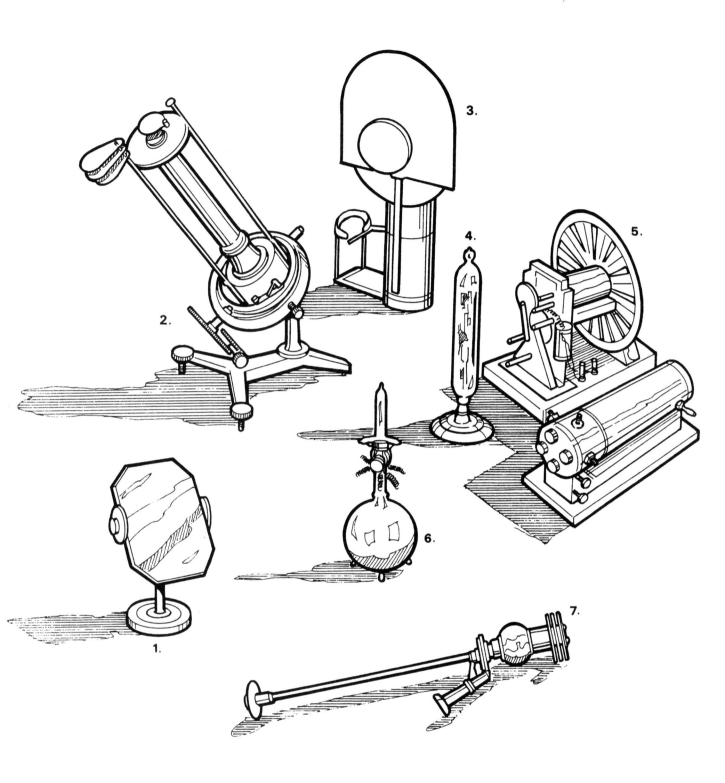

EARLY TWENTIETH-CENTURY ASTRONOMICAL INSTRUMENTS

While astronomers were gazing at the planets of our solar system through refracting and reflecting telescopes, other scientists were studying the heavens with a different array of instruments. Shown above are some of these early twentieth-century tools, which were used to study the properties of light, and other electromagnetic radiation that reached the earth from our sun.

1. Sunspot Mirror—This was used to observe the dark spots of cooler nuclear material on the surface of the sun.

2. Silver Disk Pyrheliometer—This was used to measure the components of sunlight.

3. Light Sensitive Cell.

4. Crookes Tube—This contains a light-sensitive "paddle wheel," turned by solar radiation.

5. Revolving Sector Radiometer—This was used to measure the luminosity of the sun.

6. Bolometer—This was a component for holding the water necessary to cool a device in order to measure radiant heat.

7. Pyrheliometer—This was used for balloon work.

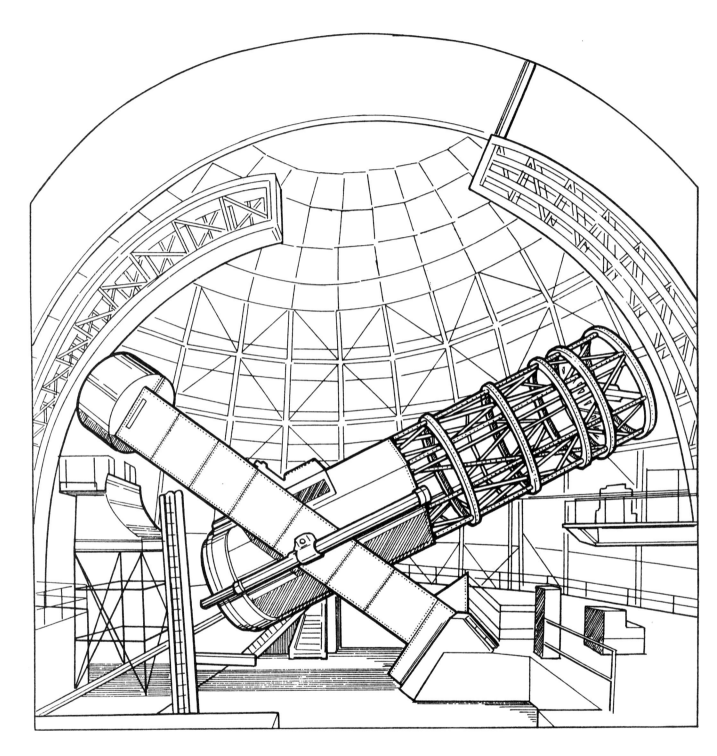

HOOKER 100-INCH REFLECTOR TELESCOPE (1917)

As technology began its rapid advance during the twentieth century, telescope design progressed as well. Major observatories competed with each other to build the largest and most powerful telescope. In California, atop Mt. Wilson overlooking Los Angeles, a sixty-inch mirror reflector was constructed in 1908. This was joined by the first "super scope" in 1917: the Hooker 100-inch reflector, designed by famed telescope engineer George Ellery Hale, and named after John D. Hooker, a wealthy industrialist who financed the project. The Hooker telescope

was crucial to the work of astronomers Edwin Hubble and Milton Humason in their pioneering observations of galaxies—the huge collections of stars like our own Milky Way.

For many years the Hale telescope, situated on Mt. Palomar in California, held the record for being the world's most powerful telescope. Dedicated in 1948 and named after George Ellery Hale, its primary reflecting mirror was an immense 200 inches in diameter.

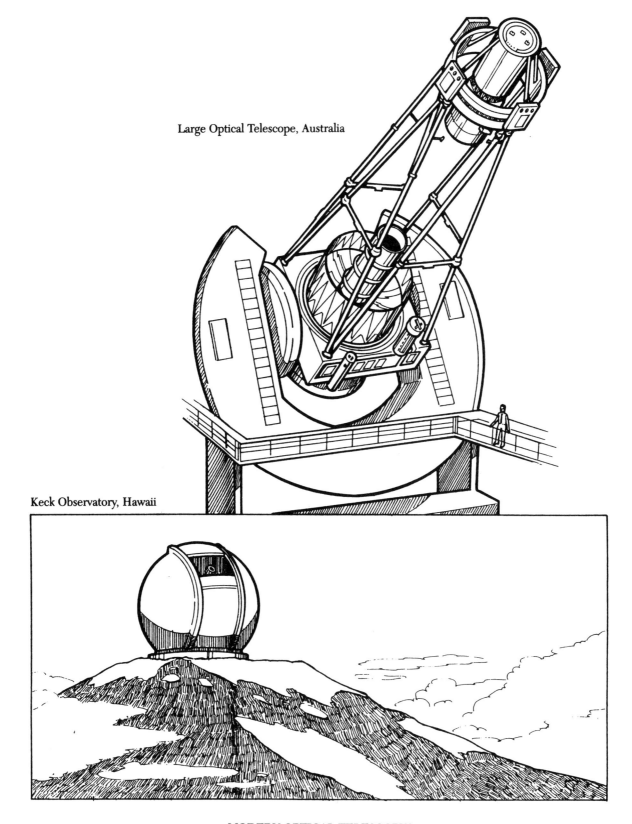

Large Optical Telescope, Australia

Keck Observatory, Hawaii

MODERN OPTICAL TELESCOPES

Today's astronomers use two types of telescopes for their work. Refracting or reflecting telescopes are used by scientists who view distant images in the night sky within the visible light spectrum, i.e., light that is visible to the human eye. However, this range of the electromagnetic spectrum is only a small portion of the total energy output of the universe. Astronomers who study the stars outside the visible light range use "radio telescopes."

Shown above is the Anglo-Australian optical reflector telescope located in Siding Spring, Australia. It has a primary mirror diameter of 156 inches. Observatories using optical telescopes are almost always located in areas far from densely populated areas with their attendant air pollution. Deserts and mountaintops are ideal sites for these observatories. The one shown above is situated on the Hawaiian volcanic mountain of Mauna Kea, at an altitude of 13,600 feet. The Keck reflecting telescope which it houses has the world's largest reflecting mirror—394 inches in diameter.

The sharpest and most powerful telescope currently in use is the Hubble Space Telescope. It does not have to deal with peering through the earth's thick and sometimes murky atmosphere. It will be discussed in greater detail on page 41.

15

Radio Telescope at the Very Large Array, New Mexico

RADIO TELESCOPES

Most of the energy in the electromagnetic spectrum of our universe is outside the visible light range. This energy includes ultraviolet and x-rays, cosmic rays, infrared rays, and radio waves. The name "radio waves" is somewhat misleading since they emit no sound, but are simply a long amplitude form of natural radiation from the stars, galaxies, and other energy sources in the universe.

The first radio telescope was built by amateur astronomer and radio operator, Grote Reber, in 1936. He based his instrument on the discovery of naturally occurring radio waves made by Bell Laboratories scientist, Karl Jansky, in 1931. Reber's first telescope was primitive and flimsy, and could only receive weak radio signals. But over time, larger, more powerful and complex radio telescopes were constructed around the world. Radio telescopes not only study distant objects in the night sky,

but also function together for deep space tracking and as a communications network for spacecraft which have been launched from earth to other planets in our solar system.

The most powerful radio telescope in use today is shown above. It is one of twenty-seven separate radio-dish antennas connected by computer, arranged in a huge "Y" shape covering seventeen square miles. It is called the Very Large Array (VLA), and is located near Socorro, New Mexico. Each radio-dish receiver is seventy-five feet in diameter. The largest single-dish radio telescope is located in a mountain valley in Arecibo, Puerto Rico. Its massive stationary dish measures 1,000 feet in diameter. It is steered—or directed—by means of a single movable focus mechanism suspended above the dish.

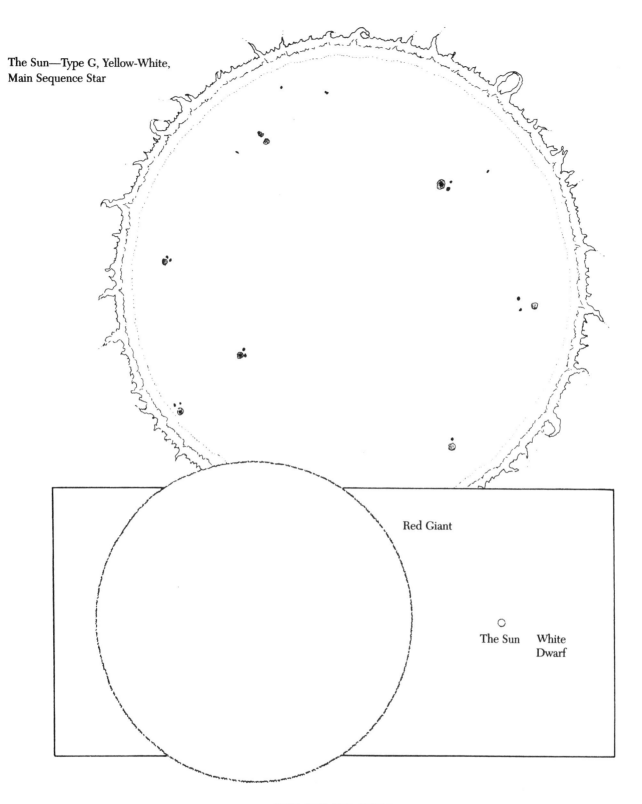

The Sun—Type G, Yellow-White, Main Sequence Star

Red Giant

The Sun   White Dwarf

THE SUN AND STARS

Stars are the engines that power the universe, including our own sun which enables life to exist on earth. In turn, all stars are powered by nuclear fusion, the process in which hydrogen atoms are fused by heat and pressure into helium atoms. This reaction gives off immense amounts of energy in the form of light and heat.

There are many different types of stars. Our sun is classified as a medium-sized, yellow-white, type G main sequence star, which began its life approximately 5 billion years ago. It is 870,331 miles in diameter, making it the largest object in our solar system by far. It is comprised of 73 percent hydrogen and 24 percent helium, with traces of many other elements. The surface temperature of the sun is around 10,000°F, while its interior temperature averages 27,000°F. The dark brown splotches on the sun's surface, so-called "sunspots," are cooler areas of only around 6,000°F.

Our sun is expected to remain stable for another 5 billion years, until it undergoes the stellar "dying process," eventually becoming a cold, planet-sized "brown dwarf" star. As part of the sun's final evolution, it will flare up into a massive "red giant" star, many times its present size, bringing it into closer proximity with the earth. This will dry up the oceans and extinguish all life on our planet. After its red giant phase, the sun will begin to collapse in upon itself, becoming first a white dwarf star, then a brown dwarf, and finally a black dwarf. Some stars collapse even further to form the most powerful gravitational force in the universe—a black hole.

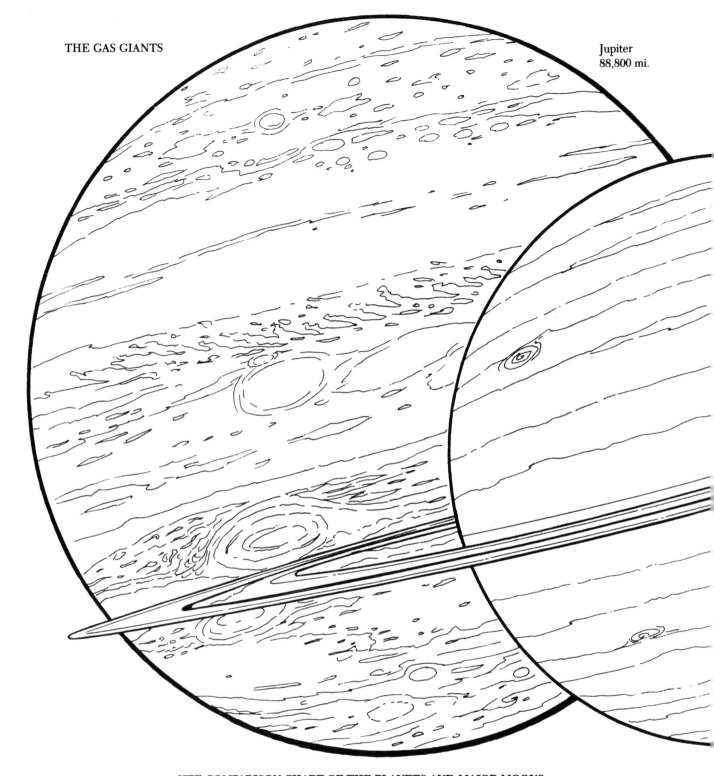

SIZE COMPARISON CHART OF THE PLANETS AND MAJOR MOONS

There are nine planets in our solar system. Other celestial bodies in orbit around our sun are the asteroids, the periodic comets, and dozens of moons—both large and small—that circle many of the planets.

Astronomers classify planets into two main types: the "terrestrial planets," and the "gas giants." The four inner planets, so-called because they are closest to the sun, are terrestrial. They are Mercury, Venus, Earth, and Mars. These planets have a rocky, solid surface, like the earth. Some have a gaseous atmosphere, while others have no atmosphere at all. Orbiting between Mars and Jupiter is a belt of irregularly shaped planetoids (or minor planets) and rocky fragments, known as the asteroids.

The four "outer planets" are the gas giants. They are Jupiter, Saturn, Uranus, and Neptune. The gas giants do not have a solid surface like the terrestrials. They are composed of a very deep outer atmosphere of gases such as hydrogen and helium, an intermediate layer of liquid gases, and an inner core of liquified metallic hydrogen. These layers are all bound together by the powerful gravity created by their immense size.

The ninth and most distant planet is tiny Pluto. There is some question among astronomers as to whether Pluto is actually a planet or an escaped moon of Neptune. Another theory under discussion is whether Pluto might be one of a different type of planet known as an "icy dwarf." Pluto, its sizeable companion moon, Charon, and Neptune's large moon, Triton, may all be members of this new planetary classification.

Jupiter and Saturn have the largest moons as well as the greatest number of them. Jupiter's satellite, Ganymede, is the biggest moon in the solar system. With a diameter of 3,278 miles, its size is greater than

18

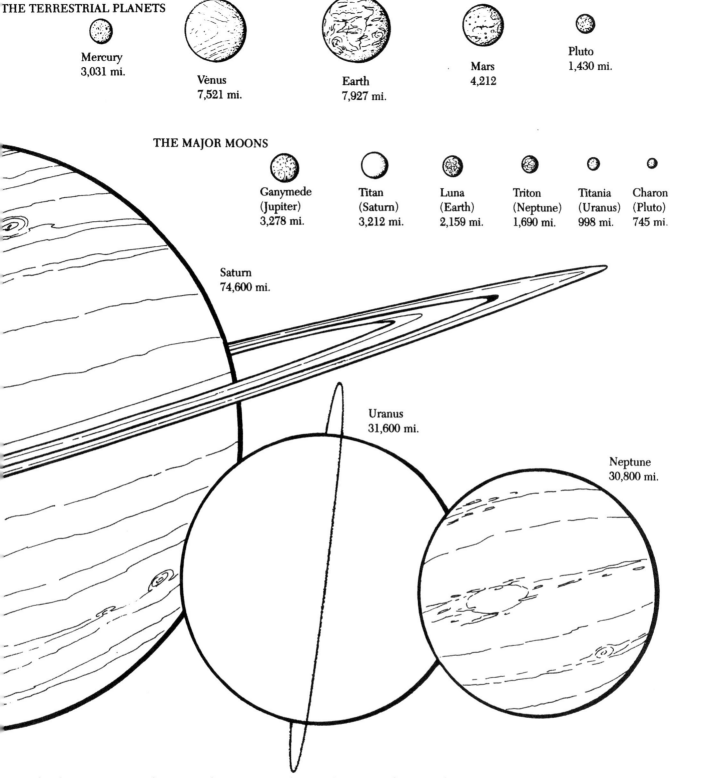

THE TERRESTRIAL PLANETS

Mercury
3,031 mi.

Venus
7,521 mi.

Earth
7,927 mi.

Mars
4,212

Pluto
1,430 mi.

THE MAJOR MOONS

Ganymede
(Jupiter)
3,278 mi.

Titan
(Saturn)
3,212 mi.

Luna
(Earth)
2,159 mi.

Triton
(Neptune)
1,690 mi.

Titania
(Uranus)
998 mi.

Charon
(Pluto)
745 mi.

Saturn
74,600 mi.

Uranus
31,600 mi.

Neptune
30,800 mi.

the planets Mercury or Pluto. Titan, the giant moon of Saturn, has a thick atmosphere of nitrogen, the primary component of the earth's atmosphere. It is only slightly smaller than Ganymede at 3,212 miles in diameter. Our own moon, at 2,159 miles in diameter, is roughly one-quarter the size of the earth, a very large satellite when considered in relation to the size of its planet. The planet Uranus has a sizeable moon, Titania, at 998 miles, and Neptune has a large moon, Triton, about 1,690 miles in diameter. Little Pluto is unique in that its companion, Charon, has a diameter of 745 miles, fully one-half the size of the planet. Some scientists think that Charon is not a moon at all, but along with Pluto, part of a double planet system.

Finally, the last members of our solar system are the icy comets which revolve around the sun in huge elliptical orbits that bring them close to the sun and inner planets only over lengthy time periods. The most famous comet, Halley's Comet, completes an orbit every 76 years.

PLANETARY DIAMETERS:
Mercury—3,031 miles
Venus—7,521 miles
Earth—7,927 miles
Mars—4,212 miles
Jupiter—88,800 miles
Saturn—74,600 miles
Uranus—31,600 miles
Neptune—30,800 miles
Pluto—1,430 miles

19

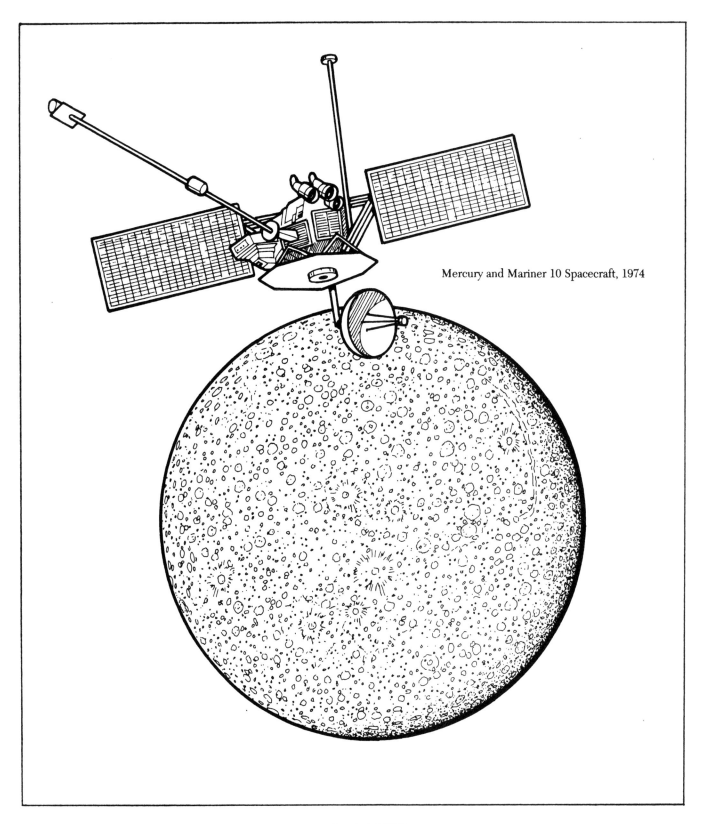

Mercury and Mariner 10 Spacecraft, 1974

PLANET MERCURY

Orbiting the sun at an average distance of 43,000,000 miles, Mercury is the closest planet to our parent star. It makes a complete orbit around the sun in just eighty-eight days (a Mercurian "year"). Mercury is the smallest of the inner terrestrial-type planets with a diameter of only 3,031 miles. Although it has the shortest year—the equivalent of eighty-eight earth days—Mercury has a very long planetary "day" due to its slow rotation. A complete Mercurian day equals fifty nine earth days.

Mercury has a thin atmosphere comprised only of trace elements of helium. The temperature on its surface ranges from a blistering 620°F on the side facing the sun, to a numbingly cold –346°F on its dark side.

The surface of the planet is scarred by thousands of meteoric impact craters, cracks, and fissures. The largest single feature on Mercury is a flat plain called the "Caloris Basin." This basin is 838 miles in diameter and similar in appearance to the lunar "seas" of our own moon. Mercury is the most dense (i.e., most solid or compressed) of all the planets due to its very large, partly molten iron core.

Visited just once by an earth-launched robot spacecraft, in 1974, the American planetary probe Mariner 10 reached Mercury and passed within 12,000 miles of its surface. It relayed detailed photographs, temperature, and magnetic field information back to earth.

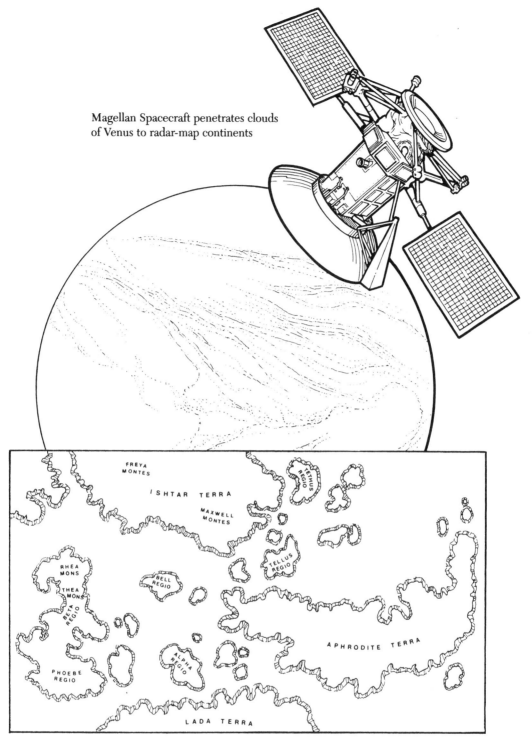

Magellan Spacecraft penetrates clouds
of Venus to radar-map continents

FREYA
MONTES

ISHTAR TERRA

TETHUS
REGIO

MAXWELL
MONTES

RHEA
MONS

BELL
REGIO

TELLUS
REGIO

THEA
MONS

BETA
REGIO

APHRODITE TERRA

ALPHA
REGIO

PHOEBE
REGIO

LADA TERRA

PLANET VENUS

Although Venus was named after the Roman goddess of love and beauty, the planet's actual features more closely resemble the medieval description of hell. It has a crushing atmospheric pressure ninety times greater than earth. Its surface temperature averages 850°F, and the atmosphere of the planet is composed of poisonous carbon dioxide gas and clouds of corrosive sulfuric acid. No earth-based life form could survive in this antagonistic environment.

Venus is the second planet from the sun and orbits at an average distance of 67,000,000 miles. Its average distance from earth is 26,000,000 miles. While it is very close to the earth in size, it does possess a slightly smaller diameter of 7,521 miles. Slow-rotating Venus has a day that lasts 243 earth days, and a Venusian year takes 224 earth days.

The degree of light reflectivity exhibited by a planet or star is called its "albedo." Because of Venus' intense albedo and its close proximity to both the sun and the earth, we usually see it as the brightest object in the night sky. It is often called the "evening star," because it begins to shine in the early evening. Unlike the stars which "twinkle" or shine with a variable degree of brightness, Venus shines steadily.

Robot spacecraft from earth have reached Venus several times. An American robot probe, the Magellan spacecraft, reached Venus in 1990. It settled into an orbit and began radar-mapping the surface through the planet's thick cloud layer. Magellan discovered several continent-sized highland plateaus surrounded by lowland plains, areas much like waterless seas. The largest of these continental land masses was named "Ishtar Terra." It covers an area of 6,700 miles by 1,900 miles. The plains and highlands of Venus are covered with thousands of meteor impact craters, as well as hundreds of dormant volcanoes. These include the massive "Montes Maxwell," which rises 39,000 feet into the Venusian sky, a full 10,000 feet higher than earth's highest peak—Mt. Everest (29,028 feet).

21

Astronaut on lunar surface with earthrise overhead

PLANET EARTH

Earth is the sole living planet of our solar system. Its distance from the sun, abundance of water, and thick atmosphere combine to create a world teeming with life. It is a geologically dynamic planet with active volcanoes and shifting "tectonic plates" (i.e., slablike sections of earth supporting the continents) making up its thin, rocky crust. At the center of our planet lies a molten-iron core which creates a strong magnetic field around the planet.

The earth orbits the sun at a distance of 93,000,000 miles. Its diameter is the largest of the inner planets at 7,927 miles. The earth takes twenty-four hours to complete a full rotation on its axis—a terrestrial day. An earth year takes 365 days for a complete cycle around the sun. The surface temperature of earth ranges from a high of 136°F to a low of −126°F.

The geography of earth is composed of seven large land masses or "continents," surrounded by vast oceans of water. These oceans cover 70 percent of our planet's surface. Located at the top and bottom of the earth are the north and south polar regions, comprised mainly of ice. The atmosphere of the earth consists primarily of nitrogen and oxygen. These gases form a one-hundred-twenty mile thick barrier that protects our planet from solar radiation and all but the largest meteoric impacts. Scientists believe that life began on earth between 2 and 3 billion years ago, starting as simple organic molecules and evolving to the complex life forms of the present.

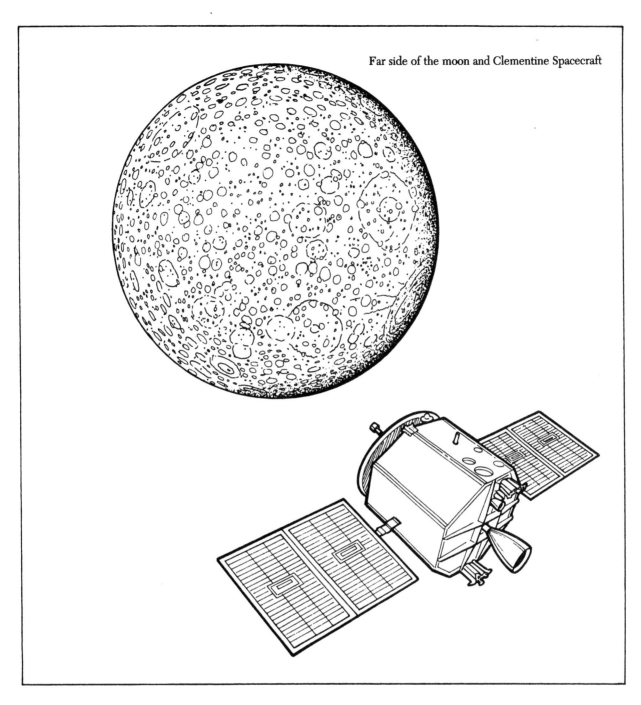

Far side of the moon and Clementine Spacecraft

LUNA, THE MOON OF PLANET EARTH

The planet earth has one large natural satellite, simply called "the moon," although it has also been referred to throughout history as "Luna," a named derived from the Latin language of the ancient Romans. It is the largest moon orbiting any of the inner terrestrial planets. The diameter of the moon is 2,159 miles, fully one-quarter the size of its parent planet. It circles the earth at a distance of 252,698 miles.

The moon is believed to have been formed several billion years ago. A current theory suggests that the earth was struck in its prehistoric past by a large planetary body, approximately the size of Mars, which blasted material into space. The fragments generated by the tremendous explosion gradually accumulated into a solid sphere due to powerful gravitational forces.

The moon has a harsh, airless environment, unsuitable for earth's life forms. The lunar temperature ranges from a high of 279°F in direct sunlight, to a low of –320°F in the dark or shadow areas. Its surface is heavily cratered, and also includes large, smooth plains called "seas." Although these seas are dry and waterless, recent evidence gathered by the Clementine robot spacecraft suggests that frozen water ice may lie in deep fissures and canyons at the moon's polar regions.

The moon became the first planetary body to be visited by human beings on July 19, 1969. The American spacecraft Apollo 11 touched down on the lunar surface with three astronauts aboard. In their protective spacesuits, these astronauts explored their landing site, and collected rocks and dust from the moon's surface. Six more lunar landings were made by Apollo astronauts during the 1970s.

The most recently launched robot probe to the moon—Lunar Prospector—is equipped with sensitive instruments specifically designed to search for water. If significant quantities of ice are found at the lunar poles, it would be a major step forward toward colonizing the moon. In addition to being necessary for the sustenance of human life, water can also be broken down into its constituent elements—hydrogen and oxygen—with oxygen providing an air supply for lunar explorers. In addition, the elements of hydrogen and oxygen are the principal ingredients for rocket fuel, which—if present—would enable the moon to become a "filling station" by supplying the necessary fuel to spacecraft for further exploration of the solar system. These factors gain importance when considered in the context of an early twenty-first century manned mission to Mars.

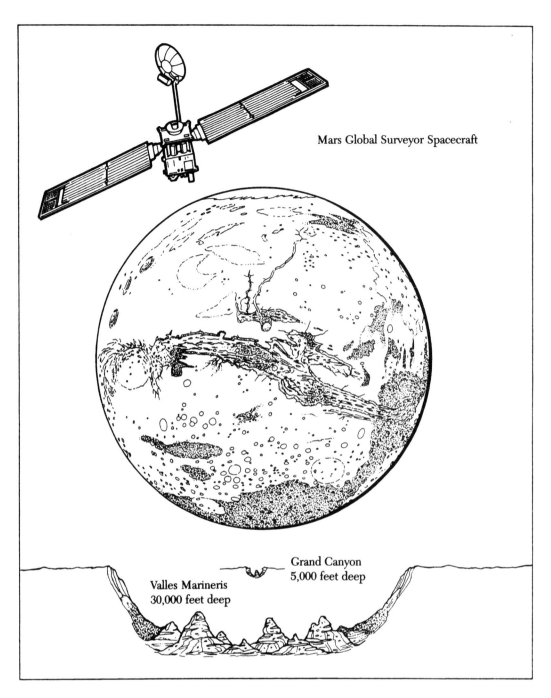

Mars Global Surveyor Spacecraft

Grand Canyon
5,000 feet deep

Valles Marineris
30,000 feet deep

MARS VIEW WITH "VALLES MARINERIS" SHOWN

Mars is a planet with a spectacular geological environment. Shown in the above view is the awe-inspiring Grand Canyon of Mars, the "Valles Marineris" or Valley of the Mariners. It was named for a series of American robot space probes which took the first detailed photographs of this immense gorge that runs across the face of Mars. Its physical dimensions dwarf our own Grand Canyon, as shown by the illustration offered for comparison. The channels and canyons of the Valles Marineris follow a course over 3,000 miles long and 450 miles wide. By comparison, the Grand Canyon of Arizona is just 217 miles long and 18 miles wide. The steep cliff walls in some areas of the Valles Marineris rise an astonishing 30,000 feet from floor to canyon rim, while the Grand Canyon is just 5,000 feet deep at its lowest point.

Mars orbits the sun at an average distance of 141,500,000 miles. At that distance, it does not receive very much solar heat energy, making it a cold, dry planet. Although its temperature can reach a balmy 60°F during a summer day on the Martian equator, it can also plunge to a frigid −190°F in the evenings. At 4,212 miles, the planet's diameter is roughly half that of the earth. Mars is located at an average distance of 48 million miles from the earth.

Mars has a very thin atmosphere—about one percent as thick as the earth's. This unsubstantial Martian air is composed mainly of carbon dioxide, nitrogen, and very small traces of oxygen. Some scientists believe that Mars had a much thicker atmosphere in its ancient past—which would have trapped some of the solar radiation it received—suggesting it was once a much warmer planet. Recent evidence has been found to support the theory that Mars had rivers and seas of liquid water in this warmer period. Scientists theorize that Mars lost its atmosphere because of its relatively small size which, in turn, could not generate enough gravity to retain the gases. Without a conducive atmosphere, Mars lost its warmth and water, and became the cold and barren desert planet of today.

Shown at the top of the illustration above is the Mars Global Surveyor robot spacecraft. It reached Mars in November of 1997 after a year-long space flight. It is programmed to survey and map the surface of the planet during a two-year orbit. It will yield the closest and most detailed views of Mars ever obtained.

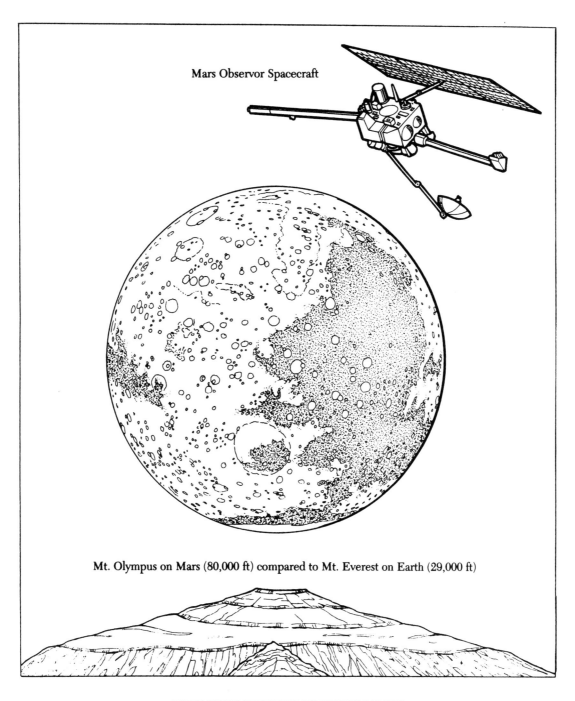

Mars Observor Spacecraft

Mt. Olympus on Mars (80,000 ft) compared to Mt. Everest on Earth (29,000 ft)

MARS VIEW SHOWING "OLYMPUS MONS"

Mars has another geological feature of immense size—i.e., the extinct shield volcano, "Olympus Mons" (Mt. Olympus). A shield volcano is so named for its circular shape, similar to the warrior's shield. This stunning volcanic formation rises to a height of over 80,000 feet, making it by far the highest mountain in our solar system. At its circular base, the mountain is 350 miles in diameter. The caldera, or center "mouth" of the volcano, is 54 miles wide. Mt. Everest rises to a relatively puny 29,000 feet over the Himalayan mountain range by comparison.

Olympus Mons is located in the Amazonis Planis region of Mars. In the Tharsis region nearby, there are three other great shield volcanoes in a row: Arsia Mons, Pavonis Mons, and Ascraeus Mons. All three rise higher than Mt. Everest. Geologists believe that the same low gravity factor which caused Mars' loss of atmosphere, promoted the colossal heights of these mountains. On earth, mountains of such size would collapse under their own weight.

The "Tharsis Bulge" is another notable feature of the Martian terrain. It is a large area in the southern hemisphere that is one and one-half times higher than the planet's northern hemisphere. Scientists conjec-ture that the bulge was caused by the impact of a huge celestial object millions of years ago striking the side opposite.

Mars has always been known as the "red planet," because of its red-dish color which is caused by rocks, sand, and dust containing large amounts of red-orange iron oxide—otherwise known as rust. There are also large dark areas on the Martian surface which periodically change size and shape. Past speculation suggested the presence of vegetation which grew and withered with the seasons. We now know that these are areas of black rock and sand that change shape due to the powerful windstorms which regularly blow across the planet. In 1971, the Mariner 9 space probe encountered the planet when it was completely enshrouded in a global sandstorm.

Shown at the top of the illustration is the Mars Observer robot space probe. Launched in 1992, it reached the planet in August of 1993. As it began orbital maneuvers designed to allow it to photo-map the entire Martian surface, radio contact was lost. It is assumed that mechanical problems caused the spacecraft's failure, but its actual fate is unknown.

25

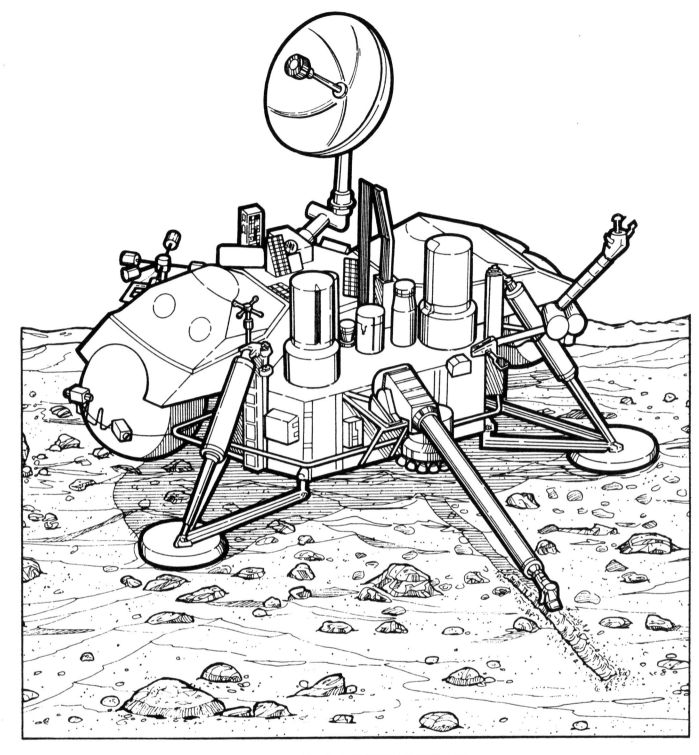

VIKING LANDER ON MARTIAN SURFACE

The exploration of Mars took a major step forward when two American robot spacecraft, Viking 1 and 2, made successful soft-landings on the Martian surface. Viking 1 touched down on the Plains of Gold region in July of 1976, and Viking 2 landed at the Utopia Plains region in September of 1976.

The spacecraft were equipped with cameras and an array of other instruments designed to gather data about Mars. The cameras provided the first close-up color photos of the surface geology of the planet. Perhaps the most important instrument on board the landers was a self-contained biology laboratory, built to sample soil around the landing site for signs of organic life. The tests conducted were inconclusive, with some results suggesting chemical reactions characteristic of organic life, and other tests contradicting those conclusions.

Another discovery about possible Martian life was made in August of 1996. A rocky meteorite found on the frozen ice fields of Antarctica was found to have originated on the planet Mars. Sometime in Mars' ancient past, this rock as well as other fragments were blasted into space by a large meteor impact on the planet. Over a period of millions of years, the rock drifted through space until it was caught by the earth's gravitational field, finally making its way through the earth's atmosphere, and crash-landing in Antarctica about 13,000 years ago. The rock was examined and analyzed by planetary geologists for several years, with their findings being made public in 1996: they had discovered evidence of microscopic life forms embedded in the rock. Not all scientists agreed that this evidence was conclusive; some believed the possibility existed that the microbic fossils were of earthly origin. Further studies of the rock are ongoing and may eventually prove conclusive. Future robot probes to Mars, as well as manned missions, will undoubtedly expand upon this discovery and investigation.

THE MYSTERY OF THE "FACE" ON MARS

Another geological discovery on the planet's surface has lent considerable mystery and excitement to speculation about life on Mars. A hitherto unseen formation was photographed in the Cydonia region by the Mariner and Viking space probes when they orbited the planet. In certain light conditions, this structure bears a striking resemblance to a helmeted human face. Surrounding the "face" are other geological formations which suggest pyramid shapes. The face itself has been analyzed by many scientists with various theories as to its origin.

Most scientists believe it is a natural rock formation that the human eye naturally interprets as something recognizable—such as a human face. But there is a segment of the scientific community that believes it is an artificially constructed monument (that is, in the sense of not being brought into being by nature), clearly implying the existence of an intelligent civilization sometime in Mars' history. Certain studies have shown remarkable mathematical and geological consistencies in the formation, its placement, and the surrounding structures. Its dimensions—if artificial—are staggering: it is one mile long, one mile wide, and 1,500 feet high. The facial structure is very symmetrical, with a distinct resemblance to the human countenance.

This mystery of this structure's origins—natural or artificial— might have been solved in 1993 when the Mars Observer spacecraft reached the red planet. If it had gone into its photographic-mapping orbit as planned, its powerful cameras would have shown the formation in much greater detail than did earlier robot probes. Since contact with the Mars Observer was lost just as it was to begin its orbit of the planet, the solution to this mystery will have to wait until the Mars Global Surveyor begins its photo-mapping mission scheduled for 1998.

PATHFINDER/SOJOURNER SPACECRAFT ON MARTIAN SURFACE

On July 4, 1997, Mars was again visited by a machine from earth. The American space probe, Pathfinder, with its mobile roving vehicle Sojourner aboard, bounced down onto the Martian surface in the Ares Valles region. Entering the atmosphere at 16,000 miles per hour, it was slowed in its descent first by parachutes, and on final impact by large inflated air bags, similar to those used in automobiles. It was the first time this novel method of soft-landing on a planetary surface was tried. The cushioned spacecraft made a number of bounces and rolled to a stop. It then opened up like the petals of a flower, ready to begin its investigative work.

The Pathfinder lander and the Sojourner rover were equipped with solar panels to generate electrical power. On board both vehicles were advanced color cameras. The Pathfinder had its camera mounted on a three-foot high pole that could rotate in a complete circle. With this instrument, Pathfinder took the first "panoramic" view of the Martian surface. The photos revealed large rocks, gullies, small hills, and in the distance, two mountain peaks.

The Sojourner's main instrument was a spectrometer, a device used to analyze chemical composition. After the rover rolled off its "parking spot" on the Pathfinder, it wheeled over to nearby rock formations, the spectrometer being placed against them to begin accumulating data. The rover was designed for a working life of just thirty days. It far exceeded its design parameters, as it continued measuring and transmitting data for over 100 days.

The data from many of the rock formations photographed and analyzed strongly suggested that they were swept into their current locations by massive flooding. This gave further support to the theory that

Mars was once a warmer and wetter planet. Photographic evidence from earlier Viking and Mariner Mars orbiters had already shown massive water-gouged channels on the surface, some as wide as ninety miles. At some time in Mars' distant past, global flooding caused by unknown forces had occurred. This remains yet another mystery to be solved by future missions to the planet.

Although Mars is a cold, dry planet and inhospitable to human life, it is possible to change its environment. Planetary geologists have suggested that Mars could be "terra-formed"—i.e., transformed into an earth-like planet. Certainly this would be a long, slow process, probably requiring a period of 200 to 300 years to accomplish. First, the planet would need to be warmed enough for primitive plant life from earth to survive. As more plants thrived on the surface, more oxygen would be released as a by-product from photosynthesis. Over the decades and

centuries, the atmosphere would gradually thicken, increasing the planet's temperature by trapping heat, much as the earth's atmosphere does. As Mars warmed, frozen water on and below its surface would melt and begin to form rivers, lakes, and seas. With abundant water, plant and animal life could flourish until, eventually, even human beings could inhabit the surface of Mars without protective gear and breathing equipment. The explorers and colonists from earth would then become the true "Martians." Although the precise methods and means by which Mars could be terra-formed have not yet been developed, they are well within the capabilities of current and future technologies.

The landing site of the Pathfinder has been named the "Carl Sagan Memorial Station," in honor of Dr. Carl Sagan—the scientist, educator, and space exploration visionary who passed away in 1996.

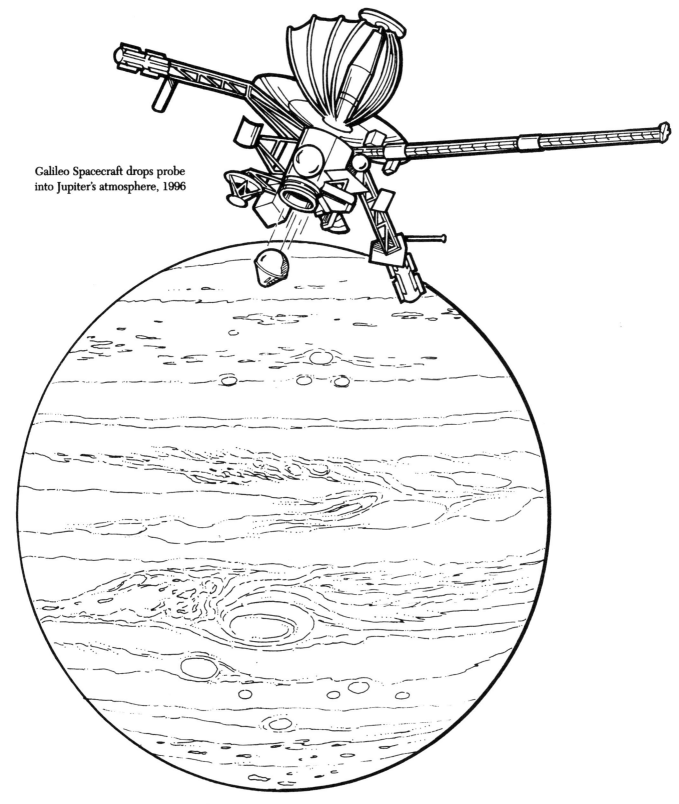

Galileo Spacecraft drops probe
into Jupiter's atmosphere, 1996

JUPITER AND ITS LARGE MOONS: GANYMEDE, CALLISTO, IO, AND EUROPA

Giant Jupiter is almost a mini-solar system in its own right. It has an immense diameter of 88,800 miles, eleven times that of the earth. Circling the planet are sixteen known moons. Four of these moons are planet-sized. The largest, Ganymede, is even bigger than the planets Mercury or Pluto. Jupiter is the first of the outer planets—the so-called "gas giants." They have no actual solid surface since they're composed of swirling gases—such as hydrogen, helium, methane, and ammonia—held together in a spherical shape by powerful gravitational forces. The chemical composition and blending of these gases give Jupiter its characteristic cloud bands of red, yellow, orange, brown, and green. Jupiter's most noticeable surface feature is its famous "Great Red Spot," a

cyclonic storm 20,000 miles long and centuries old.

Jupiter orbits the sun at an average distance of 480 million miles. Its "year"—i.e., the time it takes to make one complete solar orbit—equals twelve earth years. Conversely, Jupiter spins on its axis so fast—at 22,000 miles per hour—that its day lasts only eight earth hours. In contrast, the earth rotates on its axis at just 1,000 miles per hour. The average temperature at the outer surface of Jupiter's gas cloud layers is –200°F; its internal temperature, however, is a searing 26,000°F. This heat is produced by the tremendous pressure at Jupiter's interior regions, in turn caused by the planet's immensely powerful gravitational force. If Jupiter had been just fifty times larger, it would have gener-

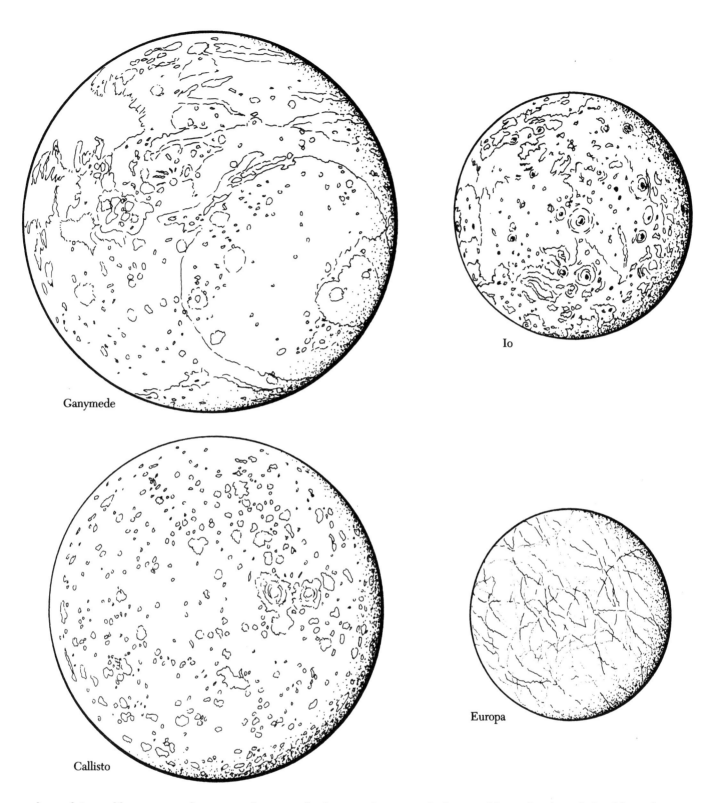

Ganymede

Io

Callisto

Europa

ated enough internal heat energy and pressure to have ignited a thermonuclear reaction, becoming a star in the process.

As mentioned earlier in these pages, Jupiter's four large moons are often referred to as the Galilean satellites since Galileo was the first to observe them. Ganymede—the largest—is composed of rock, ice, and other frozen gases, and has a diameter of 3,278 miles. Next in size is Callisto at 2,995 miles, one of the most heavily cratered objects in the solar system, its surface pockmarked by thousands of overlapping impact craters. Jupiter's next largest satellite is Io, with a diameter of 2,257 miles. This moon is in constant geological flux due to the numerous and violent volcanoes which dot its surface. These volcanoes erupt with molten sulphur, giving Io a yellow-orange appearance.

The smallest of the Galilean moons, at 1,942 miles in diameter, is Europa, one of the most fascinating objects in our solar system. Its sur-

face is completely covered by ice, heavily cracked and fissured; recent discoveries offer strong evidence that Europa has an ocean of water beneath the ice which may be warm enough to sustain life. If this is so, Europa's oceans may be the source of extraterrestrial life forms, just as earth's living creatures evolved from its oceans.

Jupiter and its moons have been visited and photographed by a number of earth space probes, including the Pioneer 10 and 11 series, and Voyagers 1 and 2. Shown in the illustration is the most recent American Jupiter probe, the Galileo spacecraft. It was launched from earth in 1989 and reached Jupiter in 1995. As Galileo orbited Jupiter, it launched a probe into the atmosphere, which recorded and transmitted data for one hour until it was destroyed by the immense heat and pressure of the planet's atmosphere.

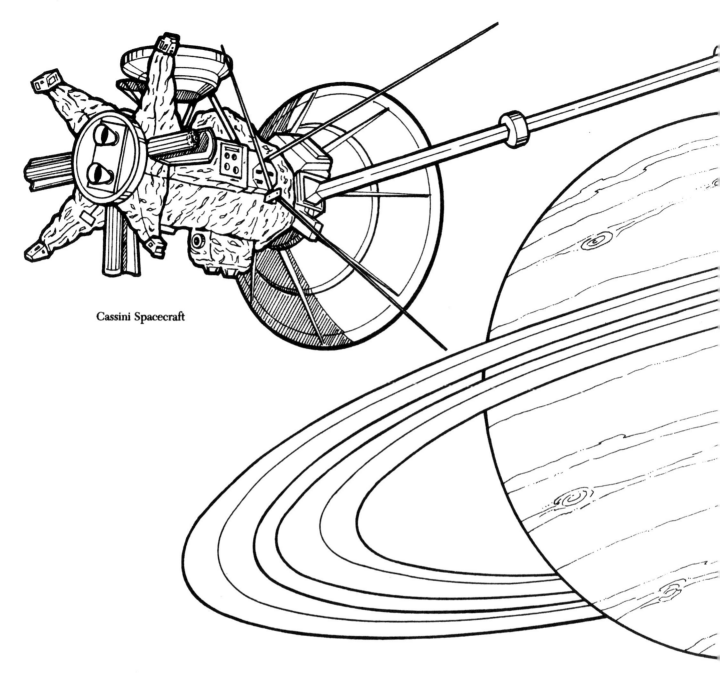

Cassini Spacecraft

SATURN AND ITS MAJOR MOONS: TITAN, IAPETUS, DIONE, TETHYS, AND MIMAS

The sixth planet in our solar system is Saturn, distinguished by its large, complex, and beautiful ring system. These rings are composed of rocks, dust, and ice, all orbiting the planet at the fantastic speed of 75,000 miles per hour. The individual pieces in the rings average no larger than one meter (thirty-nine inches). Saturn itself is the second largest planet, with a diameter of 74,600 miles. The rings begin around 7,000 miles up from the gaseous surface of the planet, and extend for another 35,000 miles into space; the diameter from ring edge to opposite ring edge is a whopping 170,000 miles.

Saturn orbits the sun at an average distance of 880,000,000 miles. At this distance, a Saturnian year takes twenty-nine earth years. Saturn spins on its axis very quickly, however, with a Saturnian day lasting only ten earth hours. Because of its great distance from the sun, Saturn receives very little heat energy, with a chilling –280°F as the average surface temperature.

In addition to its magnificent rings, Saturn has more moons than any other planet. To date, more than twenty moons have been found circling the planet. Its major moons are large and composed mainly of rock and ice. Titan—Saturn's biggest moon—is a planet-sized 3,200 miles in diameter, a very close second to Jupiter's Ganymede for the title of largest moon in our solar system. Titan is also unique in that it has a thick atmosphere composed mainly of nitrogen and methane. It may even have clouds of methane gas which rain onto the moon's surface, creating rivers, lakes, and perhaps oceans of liquid methane. Saturn's other large moons include Iapetus, with a diameter of 905 miles, and an unknown dark material covering a complete hemisphere of the satellite; Dione at 695 miles in diameter, Tethys at 650 miles, and Mimas with a diameter of 242 miles. Mimas is marked with a huge impact crater, eighty miles wide, fully one-quarter the size of the moon itself. Sometime in its ancient history, Mimas must have been struck by a gigantic celestial object such as an asteroid, comet, or planetoid.

The spacecraft shown approaching Saturn is the Cassini robot probe. It was named for the seventeenth-century astronomer, Gian Domenica Cassini, who discovered four of Saturn's moons. The Cassini probe was launched from earth in 1997, and will reach Saturn in the year 2004. It will orbit the planet while taking photographs and gathering other data to transmit back to earth. It will also drop a smaller spacecraft, the Huygens planetary probe, into the atmosphere of cloud-shrouded Titan. Perhaps it will discover what kind of surface lies below the dense cloud layer of this large moon. This smaller probe was named after Dutch astronomer, Christian Huygens, who discovered Titan in 1655.

Titan

Iapetus

Dione

Tethys

Mimas

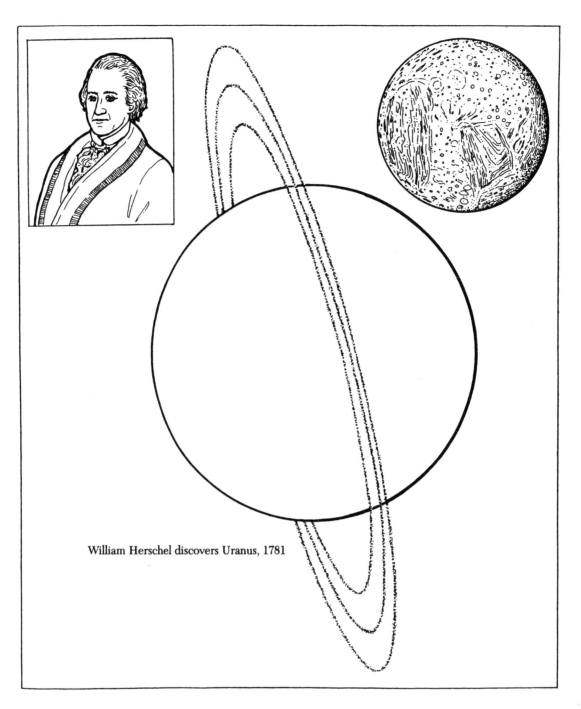

William Herschel discovers Uranus, 1781

PLANET URANUS AND ITS MOON MIRANDA

The next planet in the solar system is Uranus, the seventh planet from the sun, and the third largest of the "gas giant" planets of the outer solar system. The planet's diameter is 31,600 miles, and it orbits the sun at an average distance of 1,862,480,000 miles, which makes a Uranian year equivalent to eighty-four earth years.

Uranus has a featureless blue-green appearance but exhibits some other unusual characteristics. The planet rotates on its axis in a vertical direction of nearly ninety degrees, unlike the other planets which spin horizontally. Scientists theorize that at some point in Uranus' past, it was struck by another celestial body at least as large as the planet Mars. This collision literally knocked the planet onto its side, causing the unusual direction of its rotation. Uranus makes a complete rotation on its axis—a Uranian day—in seventeen earth hours.

Another distinctive feature of Uranus is the thin, dark ring system which orbits the planet vertically. The rings are composed of dark rock and ice, and are all but invisible from the earth. The Voyager deep-space probe discovered these rings as it passed the planet during its mission in 1986.

Uranus also has a number of large satellites. The biggest, Titania, is 998 miles in diameter. The other large moons are Oberon at 960 miles, Umbriel at 740 miles, and Ariel at 720 miles. One of Uranus' smaller moons, Miranda—at just 300 miles in diameter—exhibits some very strange surface features. As photographed by the Voyager, Miranda displayed large streaks, fissures, and chevron-shaped grooves on the surface. Scientists suspect that these markings are the result of Miranda being shattered by a collision with an asteroid or comet. Over time, the moon reformed itself through the gravitational attraction of the remaining fragments and chunks. A striking feature of this jumbled landscape are sheer cliffs that rise over 70,000 feet above the surrounding terrain, a colossal physical dimension unparalleled by any earthly phenomena.

Uranus was the first of the outer planets to be detected during the period of the modern historical record. It was discovered by the English astronomer, William Herschel, in 1781 (shown above). The inner planets of the solar system have been known and observed since ancient times. Herschel was also the first to identify clusters of stars, which he termed "island universes," and which we now know as galaxies.

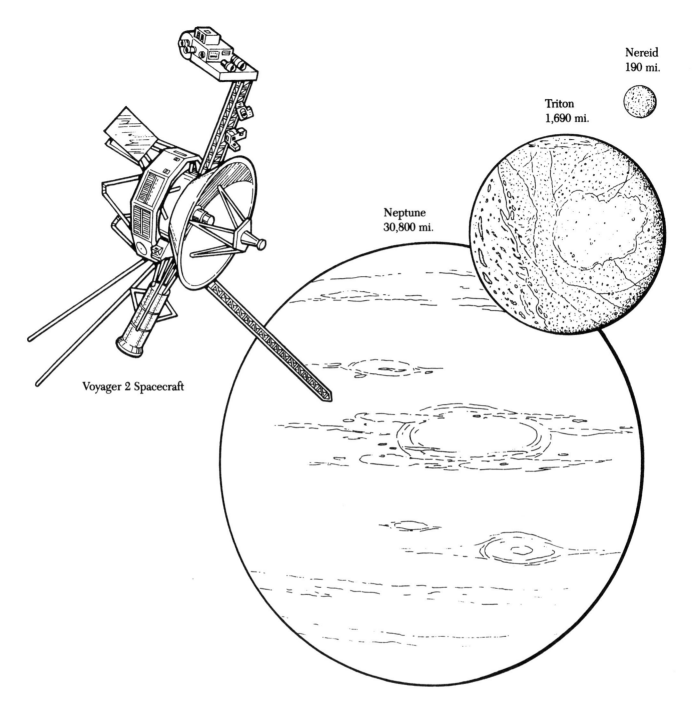

Nereid
190 mi.

Triton
1,690 mi.

Neptune
30,800 mi.

Voyager 2 Spacecraft

NEPTUNE AND ITS MOONS, TRITON AND NEREID

The last of the gas giants in the outer solar system is the planet Neptune. It has a diameter of 30,800 miles, and orbits the sun at an incredible average distance of 2,800,000,000 miles. Because of its great distance from the earth, little was known about this planet until 1989. In that year, the hardy Voyager 2 spacecraft reached Neptune after a journey of twelve years and 4.5 billion miles. As it flew within 3,000 miles of Neptune, Voyager photographed and collected data about the planet and its large moon, Triton.

The photos transmitted back to earth showed discernible cloud formations and streaks of darker blue against the bright blue sphere of the planet. It also photographed a huge cyclonic storm, much like Jupiter's Great Red Spot. It was dubbed the "Great Dark Spot" for its dark blue color. This storm is the size of the earth, with wind speeds of 400 miles per hour. White cloud streaks were also discovered moving through the planet's atmosphere at 1,500 miles per hour. Scientists nicknamed these fast-moving clouds "scooters." Neptune's bright blue color is caused by the composition of its atmosphere—mainly methane gas.

Neptune's large moon Triton—with a diameter of 1,690 miles—is unique among the planetary satellites in our solar system. It orbits the

planet in a direction opposite to Neptune's own direction of rotation, known as a "retrograde orbit." One possible explanation for this phenomenon is that Triton may not be a natural moon of Neptune, but is instead a wandering celestial body, captured by the planet's powerful gravity. Triton was found to have an atmosphere of nitrogen and methane. On the moon's surface are glaciers of frozen nitrogen and volcanoes that disgorge nitrogen ice. Triton has the coldest measured temperature of any object in the solar system: a numbing –400°F.

Neptune has one other small moon, Nereid, with a diameter of 190 miles. Its long, looping orbit suggests that it too is not a native moon, but was seized at some time in the far distant past by Neptune's strong gravitational pull. Voyager 2 also discovered a number of smaller "moonlets" orbiting Neptune, which form a broken, irregular ring system around the planet.

As of 1998, the remarkably sturdy little Voyager spacecraft, shown above, has been in space flight for twenty-one years, and has traveled a distance of 12 billion miles from earth. It still transmits data back to our planet, and scientists believe it can function for another twenty years.

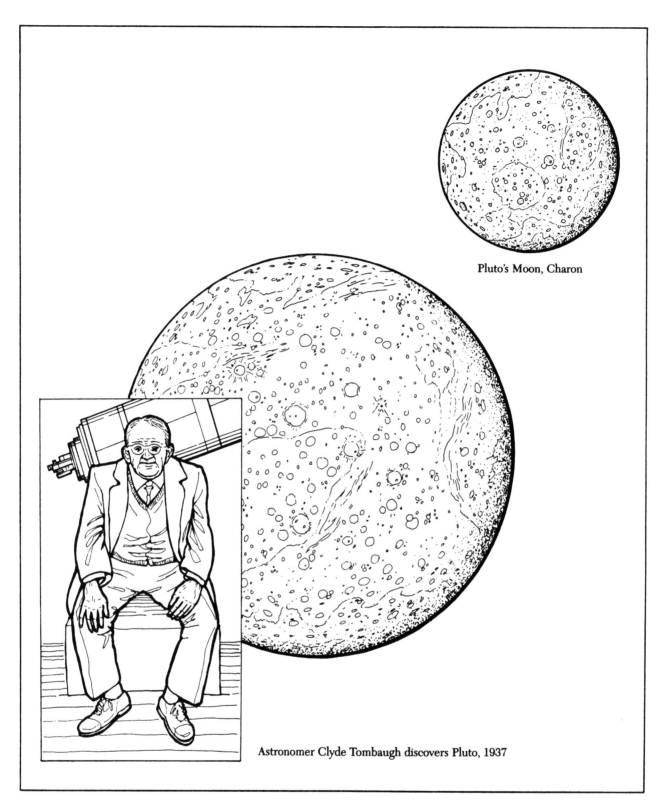

Pluto's Moon, Charon

Astronomer Clyde Tombaugh discovers Pluto, 1937

PLUTO AND ITS MOON, CHARON

Tiny Pluto is the outermost planet in the solar system, and so far distant from earth that little is known about it since no spacecraft has ever ventured there. It orbits the sun at the tremendous distance of 4.5 billion miles, which means that Pluto takes 248 earth years to make one complete solar orbit—or one Plutonian year. Pluto is also the smallest of all the planets, with a diameter of just 1,430 miles. It was also the last planet to be discovered. Astronomer Clyde Tombaugh first detected the planet in 1930 while working at the Lowell Observatory in Arizona. He is shown above in 1993 at the age of 87.

In 1978, astronomer James Christy of the U.S. Naval Observatory, discovered Pluto's moon, Charon. At 745 miles in diameter, Charon is fully one-third the size of Pluto. It is the largest moon in the solar system in relation to the size of its planet. In fact, some scientists believe that Charon may not be a moon at all, but is one part of a double-planet system with Pluto. Charon orbits Pluto at the fairly close distance of 12,000 miles.

Astronomers theorize that both Pluto and Charon are rocky, terrestrial-type worlds with ice-covered surfaces. They believe that the ice is chiefly composed of frozen methane gas. The average temperature on Pluto is -350°F. An American space probe is planned for a mission to Pluto, sometime after 2003, to photograph and collect other information about this far-distant planet for transmission back to earth.

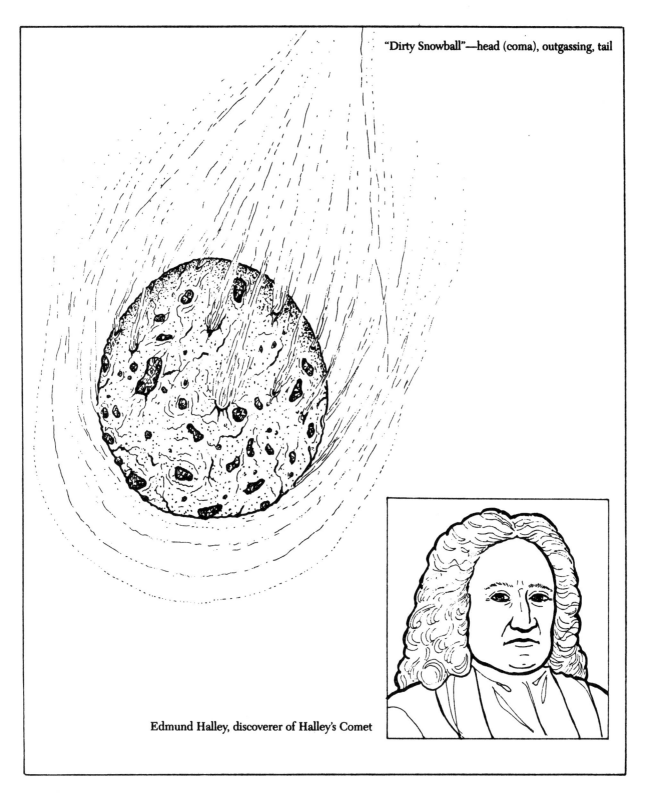

"Dirty Snowball"—head (coma), outgassing, tail

Edmund Halley, discoverer of Halley's Comet

COMETS

The icy comets are also members of our solar system. They originate in an area of the outer solar system known as the "Oort cloud"—a belt of millions of comets orbiting the sun at a distance of forty to fifty thousand times farther than the distance of the earth from the sun (known as one astronomical unit).

Comets are composed of frozen water and other gases, rocks, and dust, all mixed together in the head or "coma" of the comet. They are often referred to as "dirty snowballs." The head of a comet can range in size from ten miles to 1,000 miles in diameter. The tail of the comet, which is what we see from earth, trails behind the coma for thousands, even millions of miles. It is produced as the comet nears the sun, and the gases begin to ionize and vaporize.

The orbit of a comet around the sun is in a huge elliptical shape, looking much like a flattened circle. This brings them into the proximity of the earth and sun over regular but very long time spans. The most well-known cometary visitor is Halley's Comet, discovered in 1682 by astronomer, William Halley (shown above), and appearing every seventy-six years. Comets regularly collide with other celestial bodies such as planets and moons. The impact causes an enormous explosion resulting in the many large craters seen on numerous planetary surfaces. Many scientists believe that the earth was struck by either a comet or an asteroid 65 million years ago, causing destruction on a global scale and conditions which may have led to the extinction of the dinosaurs. This subject is discussed in greater detail on page 40.

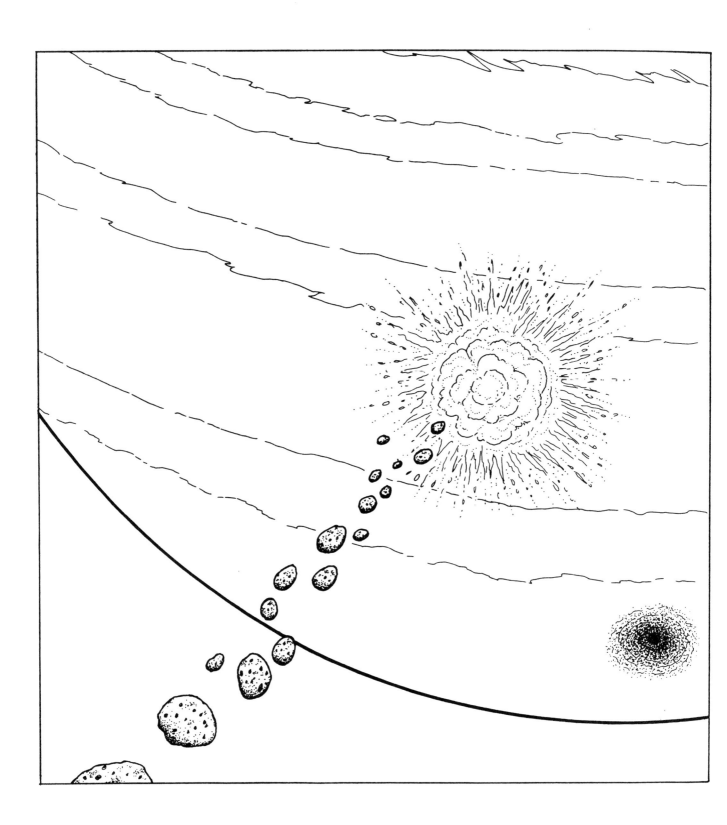

COMET SHOEMAKER-LEVY 9 IMPACTS THE PLANET JUPITER

In 1994, astronomers around the world witnessed an unprecedented event: the largest explosion ever observed as twenty-one pieces of Comet Shoemaker-Levy 9 crashed into Jupiter over a seven-day period. The comet was discovered in 1993 by astronomers Eugene and Carol Shoemaker, and David Levy. After intensive study of the comet, it was determined that it would strike Jupiter in 1994. The impacts of the various chunks of the comet were photographed by virtually all earth telescopes, the Hubble Space Telescope, and the Galileo deep-space probe orbiting Jupiter.

Originally, the comet was a single body, but as it approached Jupiter it broke into smaller fragments. The largest of these, named the "G" fragment, struck Jupiter's atmosphere at a speed of 134,000 miles per hour. The fireball created was 4,000 miles across, 1,000 miles high, and reached a temperature of 50,000°F. It hit with the explosive energy of 100 million megatons of force, 10,000 times greater than all of the earth's nuclear weapons arsenal. It left an explosive "black eye" on Jupiter that lasted for days, and was larger than the planet earth.

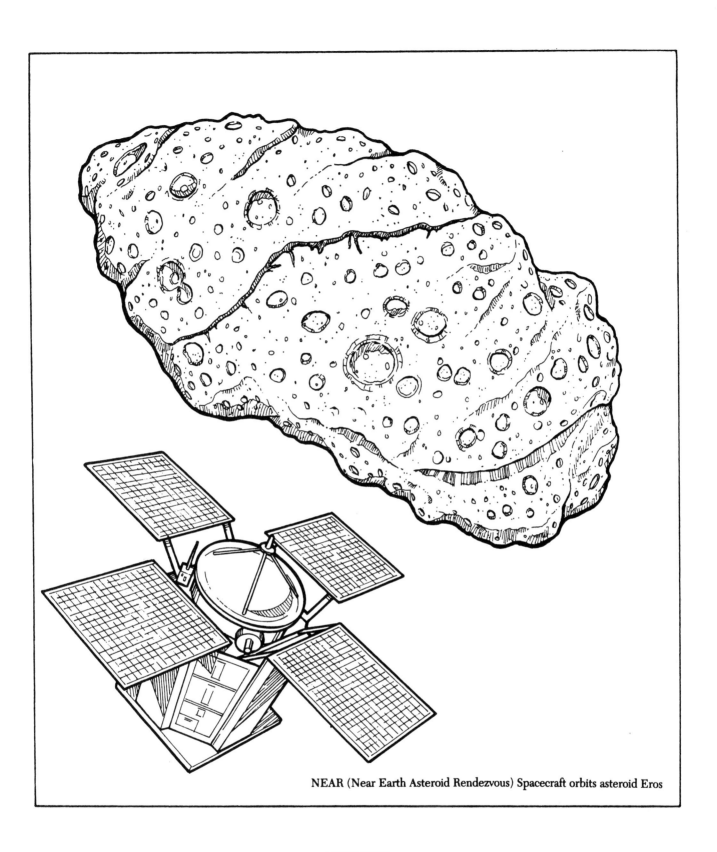

NEAR (Near Earth Asteroid Rendezvous) Spacecraft orbits asteroid Eros

ASTEROIDS

The asteroids are irregularly shaped meteoric fragments and planetoids (minor planets) that orbit the sun in a wide belt between Mars and Jupiter. Scientists have identified and catalogued over 2,000 separate asteroids. Some of the larger asteroids are Ceres, at 650 miles diameter, Pallas at 450 miles, Vesta at 370 miles, and Hygeia at 300 miles. Astronomers believe that asteroids are not fragments of a shattered moon or planet, but are stony, metallic chunks remaining from the formation of the solar system.

The spacecraft depicted above is the NEAR robot probe. NEAR stands for Near Earth Asteroid Rendezvous. It was launched from earth in 1996 and will reach the asteroid Eros in 1999. Its mission is to photograph and collect data about this twenty-two mile long rocky object. During its journey to Jupiter, the Galileo spacecraft provided the first close-up photos of these celestial bodies as it passed close to the asteroids, Gaspra and Ida. Future robot probes are scheduled for asteroid missions with the intention of firing darts into these objects to analyze their material structure.

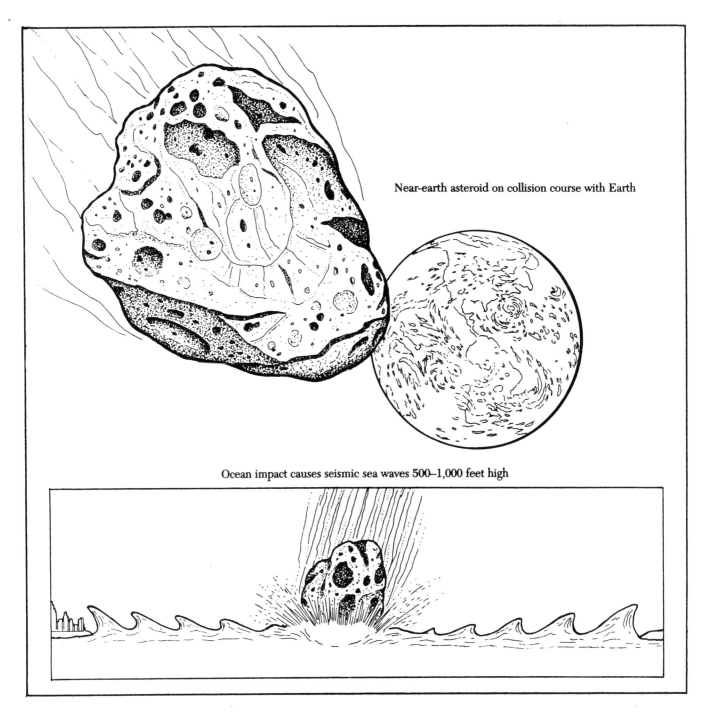

Near-earth asteroid on collision course with Earth

Ocean impact causes seismic sea waves 500–1,000 feet high

NEAR-EARTH ASTEROID COLLISION

Asteroids have periodically collided with other planets and moons in our solar system, just as comets have done. The gigantic Caloris Basin on Mercury, and the Tharsis Bulge on Mars, are both probable scars from an asteroid impact. Many of the moons in the solar system, including our own moon, display tell-tale asteroid impact craters.

The earth is not immune to being struck by one of these objects. In fact, over the last decade, scientists have discovered 1,700 asteroids which regularly pass close to our planet, called near-earth asteroids. In their ongoing search for these possible space intruders, astronomers detect about three new ones each month. If an asteroid does strike the earth, its destruction will be enormous. For example, if an asteroid one-mile wide made an ocean impact, it would create a *tsunami* (seismic sea wave) 800 feet high and destroy coastal cities within a 1,000 mile radius.

A really massive asteroid—ten miles wide or larger—strikes the earth only once every 10 million years, and causes destruction on a global scale. Using satellite radar-mapping, scientists discovered an asteroid crater on the Yucatan Peninsula in Mexico, straddling the land and the ocean floor. The diameter of this crater is 180 miles! Some scientists

believe this to be evidence of the object that struck earth 65 million years ago, ending the long reign of the dinosaur as the dominant life form on earth. In addition to the demise of the dinosaur, 70 percent of the then existing animals and plants also died out. This mass extinction was caused by the clouds of dust, smoke, and other debris thrown into the atmosphere by the explosion. The earth was completely blanketed by these clouds for over one year. The resultant loss of light for plants and heat for animals were the mechanisms for their annihilation.

Scientists believe the earth may have gone through several periods of mass-extinction in the 3-billion-year history of life on our planet. Although no fossil record exists as evidence, it is theorized that the earth may have once harbored unknown and unimagined forms of life, traces of which may have been completely wiped out.

The scientific community is currently working on methods for the early detection and destruction of earth-crossing asteroids before they strike our planet. Perhaps by the early twenty-first century we will have a system in place to protect the earth from this potential cosmic devastation.

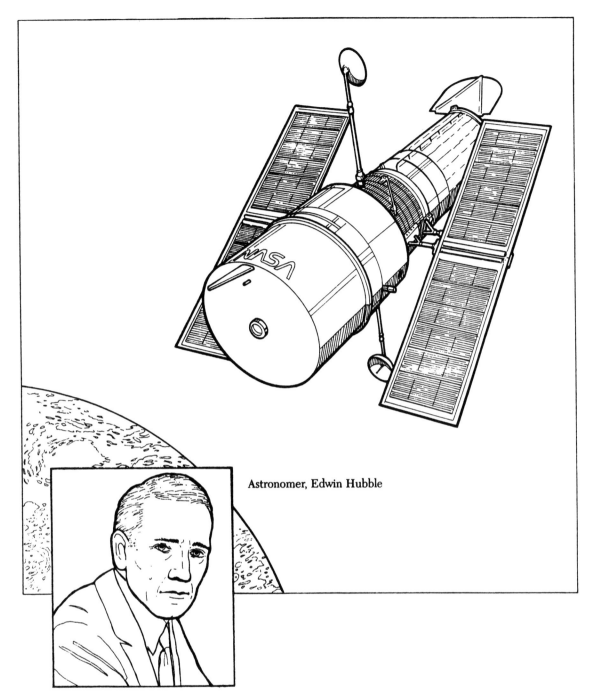

Astronomer, Edwin Hubble

HUBBLE SPACE TELESCOPE

The most powerful and sophisticated optical instrument currently in use by astronomers is the Hubble Space Telescope. It was launched into a 360 mile-high earth orbit in 1990 by the American space shuttle Discovery. High above the haze and turbulence of the earth's atmosphere, the Hubble can view the heavens with far greater clarity than earth-based telescopes. With its ninety-four inch reflecting mirror, it is able to gather both visible and ultraviolet light. A variety of on-board cameras capture the images from the mirror. The Hubble itself is forty-three feet long and weighs 25,500 pounds.

Shortly after its 1990 launch, the Hubble was found to have a slight imperfection in the main mirror, causing a major degradation of its viewing power. It was diagnosed as being "nearsighted," a disastrous condition for a telescope. A 1993 space shuttle mission corrected this optical shortcoming. Since then, the telescope has exceeded its original performance expectations. It has captured images at incredible distances from the earth with remarkable clarity. It has been most impressive in viewing distant star clusters and nebulae (or clouds of gas). What were once seen as fuzzy blobs of light, are now captured as distinct and separate spiral and pinwheel galaxies. As the Hubble looks deep into the universe, it not only sees far distant objects, but also actually looks back to an earlier time in the age of the universe. The light reaching the Hubble from these great distances has taken thousands, even millions of years to travel to earth, because the distance light travels is measured in "light-years." This constant measurement is the distance that light can travel moving at the fastest speed attainable by any known form of energy or matter: i.e., 186,000 miles per second. The closest star to our solar system (other than the sun) is Proxima Centauri. It lies a distance of 4.3 light years from the earth. Since light from this star takes 4.3 years to reach our planet, we are, in effect, seeing Proxima Centauri as it was 4.3 years ago.

The Hubble Space Telescope is named after astronomer Edwin Hubble (1889–1953), who specialized in the study of other galaxies. Using the great optical telescopes on Mt. Wilson and Mt. Palomar in California, he was able to determine that the universe was expanding, with galaxies speeding away from each other in all directions. He also discovered that a distant nebula was actually another galaxy—our closest galactic neighbor—called Andromeda. This spiral collection of stars is 4.3 MILLION light years from earth and contains over 3 billion stars.

41

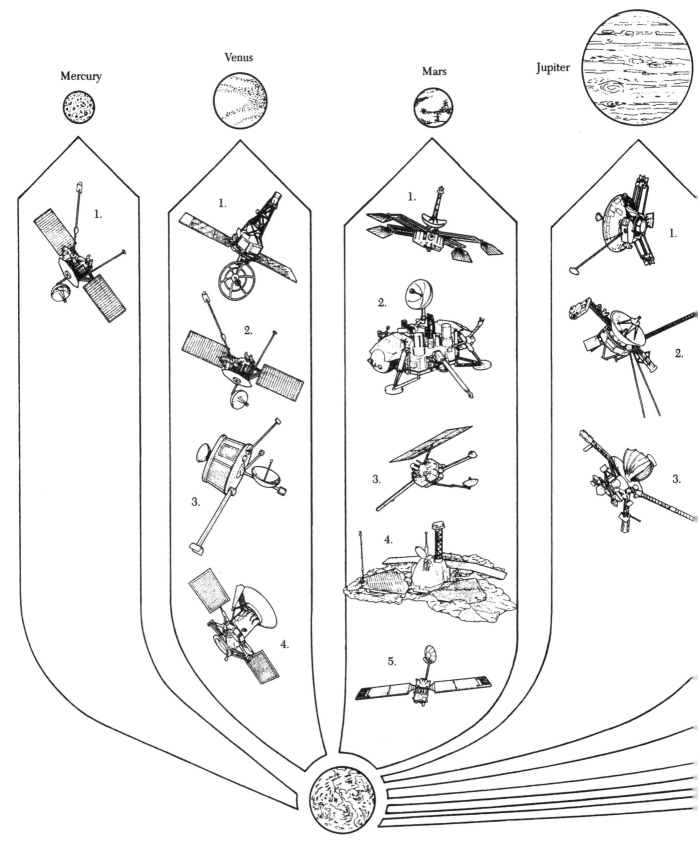

ROBOT SPACECRAFT EXPLORE THE SOLAR SYSTEM

MERCURY—Average distance from earth, 50 million miles.
1. Mariner 10—fly-by and photograph, 1974.

VENUS—Average distance from earth, 26 million miles.
1. Mariner 2—fly-by and photograph, 1962.
2. Mariner 10—fly-by and photograph, 1974.
3. Pioneer Venus—fly-by and photograph, 1978.
4. Magellan—orbit and radar-map surface, 1990–4.

MARS—Average distance from earth, 48 million miles.
1. Mariner 4 through 9—fly-by, orbit, photograph, 1965–71.
2. Viking 1 and 2—orbit, photograph, soft-land on surface, 1976.
3. Mars Observer—orbit, photograph (lost contact at beginning of orbit), 1993.
4. Mars Pathfinder/Sojourner—orbit, land on surface, photograph, Roving Vehicle spectroscopic analysis of rock formations, 1997.
5. Mars Global Surveyor—orbit, photograph, 1998–9.

JUPITER—Average distance from earth, 440 million miles.
1. Pioneer 10 and 11—fly-by, photograph, 1973, 1974.
2. Voyager 1 and 2—fly-by, photograph, 1979.
3. Galileo—orbit, photograph, drop probe into atmosphere, 1995.

SATURN—Average distance from earth, 800 million miles.
1. Pioneer 11—fly-by, photograph, 1979.
2. Voyager 1 and 2—fly-by, photograph, 1979, 1981.
3. Cassini—launch 1997, orbit, photograph, drop Huygens probe into
   atmosphere of moon, Titan, 2004.

URANUS—Average distance from earth, 1.7 billion miles.
1. Voyager 2—fly-by, photograph, 1986.

NEPTUNE—Average distance from earth, 2.6 billion miles.
1. Voyager 2—fly-by, photograph, 1989.

PLUTO—Average distance from earth, 3 billion miles.
Not yet visited by earth-launched spacecraft. Planned fly-by mission,
   post 2003.

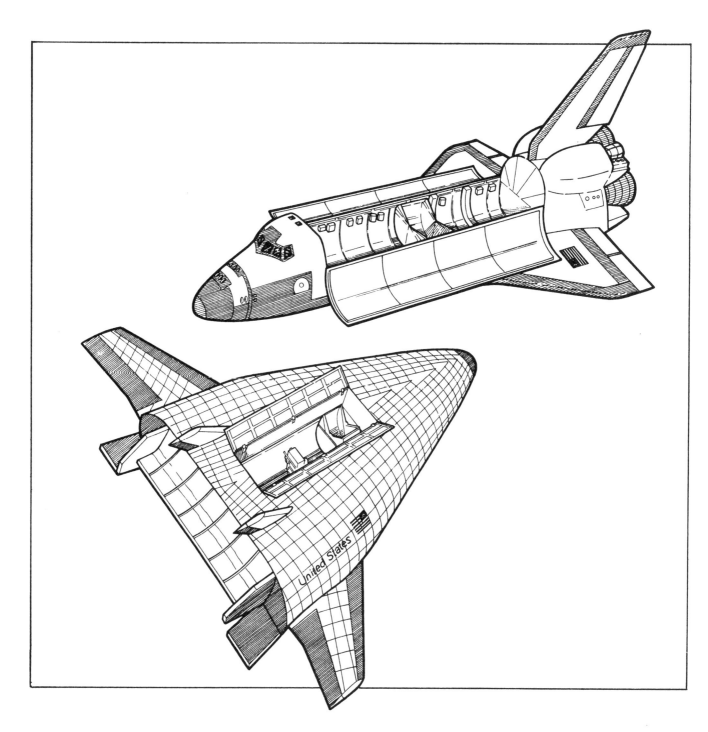

SPACE SHUTTLE AND VENTURE STAR SPACECRAFT

The American space shuttle is currently the only spacecraft that can be launched into space, orbit the earth, and land again for reuse. It is a complex vehicle that is part rocket and part airplane. First launched in 1981, the space shuttle has completed dozens of missions in its seventeen years of operation.

The spacecraft consists of an orbiting space-plane and rocket boosters used only during its launch. The orbiter has three liquid-fueled rocket engines, an 830-ton external liquid-fuel tank, and two detachable solid-fuel rocket boosters, which produce a combined thrust of 5.3 million pounds. Together with the orbiters own liquid-fuel engines of 1.1 million pounds thrust, the shuttle can carry a 65,000 pound payload into space. It can reach the speed needed for earth orbit—17,500 miles per hour—in just eight minutes! As it rests on the launch pad, the shuttle stands 184 feet tall, while the orbiter itself is 122 feet long with a seventy-eight foot wingspan.

The mid-section of the orbiter has a cargo bay sixty feet long and fifteen feet wide. It has doors that open up directly into space for launching satellites and other spacecraft. To assist in these operations, the cargo bay is equipped with a fifty-foot long, three-jointed manipulator arm. It is operated by a shuttle crew member from within the orbiters' cabin. There are four different space shuttle vehicles currently in use. They are the Columbia, Discovery, Atlantis, and Endeavor. Since they began their many missions in 1981, the orbiters have carried several hundred astronauts into space and launched dozens of satellites into the earth's orbit.

The successor to the space shuttle is called the Venture Star. It is scheduled to begin operation in 2004 as the space shuttles gradually retire from service. It is a more advanced space-plane, standing 127 feet high and weighing just over 2 million pounds. It will lift off vertically using its seven liquid-hydrogen powered engines. The Venture Star will orbit the earth, conduct its missions, and then land like a conventional airplane. It can carry a 40,000 pound payload into space at a much lower per-launch cost than the space shuttles' present cost of $500,000,000 per launch. The Venture Star will be a key element in the creation of the international space station scheduled for construction in the twenty-first century.

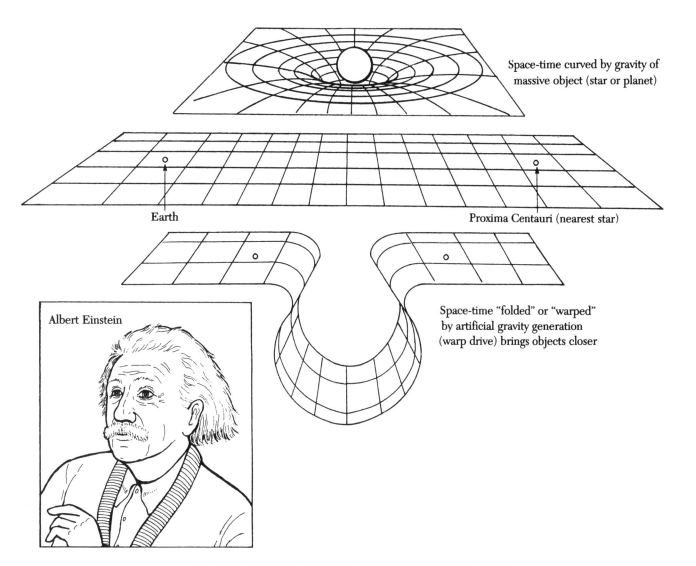

Space-time curved by gravity of massive object (star or planet)

Earth

Proxima Centauri (nearest star)

Albert Einstein

Space-time "folded" or "warped" by artificial gravity generation (warp drive) brings objects closer

ALBERT EINSTEIN AND THE NATURE OF THE UNIVERSE

As we leave the planets and moons of our local solar system, we begin the exploration of our larger "neighborhood," the Milky Way galaxy, formed from a vast, elliptically-shaped spinning disk of stars. It has a diameter of 100,000 light-years from edge to edge, and contains over 200 billion stars. It is but one of billions of other galaxies in the greater entity of the universe.

Our solar system is located on the outer rim of one of the Milky Way's spiral arms. When the night sky is viewed from a location distant from city lights, we are able to see a luminous band of stars stretching across the heavens. From our distant position on one of its outer arms, we are seeing into the star-filled center of the Milky Way.

When questions of distance and size of this magnitude are investigated, the disciplines of physics and mathematics become especially crucial to astronomy, and the name of this area of scientific endeavor changes from astronomy to cosmology. Cosmology is the study of the infinitely large, the "macro-world." It is balanced by the study of the infinitely small, the "micro-world" of basic atomic particles, known as "quantum mechanics." Both of these areas of research explore the nature of the universe.

Albert Einstein (1879–1955), the eminent theoretical physicist, possessed one of the great creative intellects in human history. His contribution to our understanding of the universe is unmatched by any other scientist. Born in Germany and later a naturalized American citizen, Einstein published two landmark papers: his special theory of relativity in 1905, and his general theory of relativity in 1915.

Einstein correctly deduced in his energy-mass equation that matter and energy are different forms of the same entity, and that a particle of matter can be converted into an enormous quantity of energy (although the means to transform energy back into matter have yet to be found). In this way, the masses of nuclei furnish the large amounts of energy supplied by nuclear reactions.

From his work, we also know that space and time are bound together into a single entity called space-time, and that the universe is described by this curved space-time, its shape being rather like the surface of an inflated balloon. This space-time curvature, in turn, is caused by the immense power of gravity, and can be affected locally by the gravitational pull of a large object. If it were possible to manipulate or bend space-time through the ability to control gravity, distant stars could be brought closer to our solar system for possible exploration.

The nature of gravity is still little understood. For example, it is not yet known whether gravity travels in wave-form like radio waves, or in particle-form like photons of light. In the forty years preceding his death in 1955, Einstein became deeply enmeshed in a search for the theory which would furnish a single explanation for all matter and energy, time and space, thus uniting them mathematically. Since he was unable to attain this goal during his lifetime, scientists today continue his quest for the so-called "unified field theory."

Einstein also discovered that as an object approaches the speed of light (186,000 miles per second)—the current "speed-limit" of our universe—time slows down for that object in relation to the surrounding area. This is called the "time-dilation" effect. For example, if an interstellar spacecraft were to travel from earth to Proxima Centauri at the speed of light, the crew would experience the passing of 4.3 years onboard the craft. On earth, however, dozens of years would have passed. To overcome the tremendous time and distance problems necessary to make interstellar travel possible, entirely new types of technology will be required. Perhaps the control of gravity will allow ships to generate "warps" in the space-time continuum, bending or folding space-time to bring two distant points closer together. It might be possible to harness the power of black holes or wormholes in order to travel through "hyperspace," leaping from one area of the galaxy to another in days, hours, or even minutes.

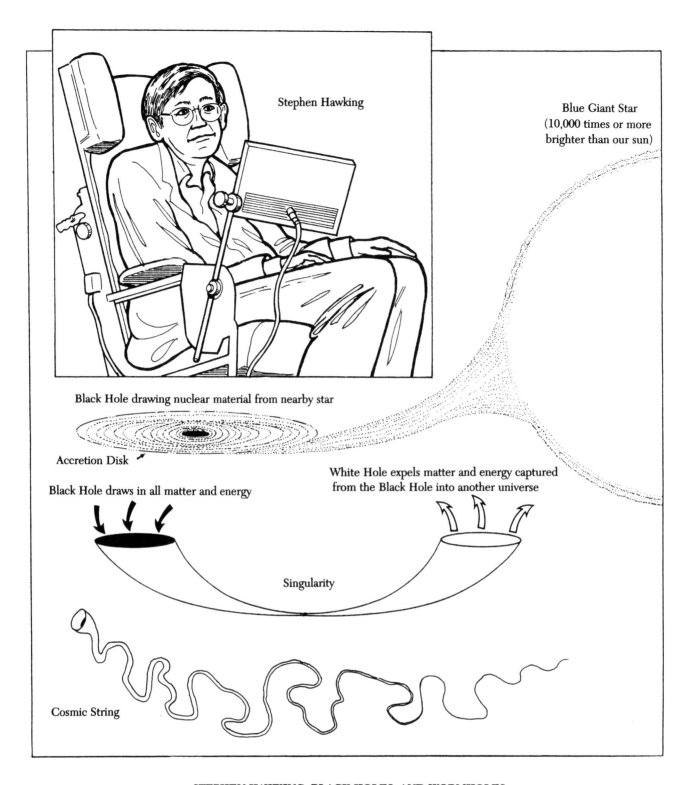

Stephen Hawking

Blue Giant Star
(10,000 times or more
brighter than our sun)

Black Hole drawing nuclear material from nearby star

Accretion Disk

Black Hole draws in all matter and energy

White Hole expels matter and energy captured
from the Black Hole into another universe

Singularity

Cosmic String

STEPHEN HAWKING, BLACK HOLES, AND WORMHOLES

The subject of black holes is one of the most exciting new topics of cosmological research. A "black hole" is the name given to the phenomenon caused by the collapse of a massive star, when it has expended its nuclear fire and shrinks into an object of such immense density and mass that no form of radiation can escape its ultra-powerful gravitational field. No light, no heat, no x-rays, or energy of any kind is emitted. At the core of a black hole is what is known as a "singularity," which—broadly interpreted and theoretically speaking—is the tunnel between two different universes through which matter and energy from the black hole is spewed out of the "white hole." These entities and their properties are at the very edge of our current knowledge of the physics of the universe. In fact, much of the information about them is so theoretical, that their very existence is still only inferred from mathematical and empirical studies.

Scientific investigations are also underway about a different, smaller version of a black hole—a "wormhole"—which could be a gateway to different parts of the universe, circumventing the awesome distance-time difficulties of traveling to these far regions. In fact, wormholes may be portals to an altogether different universe entirely, one in which our current laws of physics do not apply. Yet another relatively new theory postulates that the universe is composed of "cosmic strings," vibrating strings or loops that are far smaller than atoms. Stephen Hawking of Cambridge University in the United Kingdom is the foremost scientist today involved in the study of this cosmic esoterica, which he has also helped popularize in his best-selling book, *A Brief History of Time*.

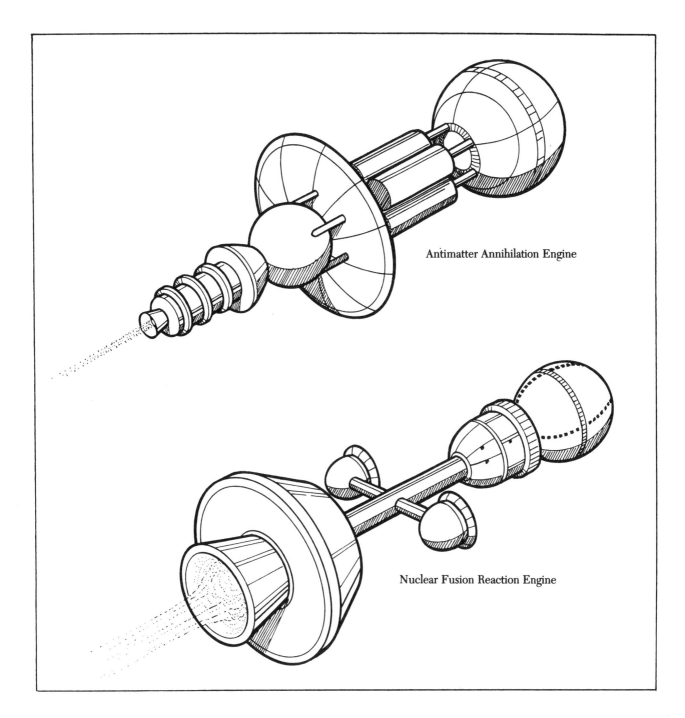

Antimatter Annihilation Engine

Nuclear Fusion Reaction Engine

FUTURE STARSHIP TECHNOLOGY

The eventual mechanism for our exploration of the Milky Way galaxy and the greater universe will be "starships." The design and construction of these interstellar spacecraft depend on developing technologies that will enable them to travel at "light speed." This velocity will be far greater than any spacecraft can currently achieve, and will need to be near, at, or in excess of, the speed of light. Today's chemical rocket engines are inadequate in terms of power and thrust to reach these speeds. Therefore, new modes of spacecraft propulsion will need to be invented, some of which are now in the theoretical research stage.

Two of the most promising technologies are antimatter annihilation engines and nuclear-fusion reaction pulse-detonation engines, both developed from concepts based on the relevant theoretical knowledge to date. Antimatter annihilation engines produce power by the reaction of antimatter and normal matter. The existence of antimatter has been known for several decades: it is a structure with the electrical charge of the atomic particles opposite from the charge of normal matter. Vast amounts of energy are produced when they combine and completely destroy—or annihilate—each other. Through the controlled process of uniting these two materials, tremendous forward thrust could be

attained. At the present time, however, only tiny amounts of antimatter can be created and safely contained. Some scientists believe that electromagnetic containment fields may eventually solve this problem.

Nuclear-fusion reaction pulse-detonation engines use the power of a nuclear-fusion bomb detonation. The explosion pushing against a huge and dense radiation shield provides forward thrust in controlled pulse detonations. Using this method, the spacecraft crew would need to be protected from the large amounts of dangerous radiation produced by the blast. These concepts in execution may be able to propel a spacecraft near the speed of light. Travel to nearby stars may then become a practical reality—as well as a very lengthy journey. Starships might need to be designed for multi-generational travel over decades or even hundreds of years.

In the meantime, the universe with all its grand and awesome mysteries awaits our further exploration. Eventually, we will travel by interstellar spacecraft to seek new knowledge among the stars themselves, when we will have realized the truth of the axiom, "What we can imagine, we can achieve."